THE VIRTUES OF
ᶜALI IBN ABI TALIB ﷺ

Jawahir Media
4370 Lawrenceville Highway NW #691
Lilburn, GA 30048
jawahirmedia@gmail.com
www.jawahirmedia.com

Cover Design: Muhammadan Press ◆ mail@muhammadanpress.com
Typesetting: Etherea Design ◆ enquiries@ethereadesign.com

ISBN 978-0-692-45702-3

THE JEWELS OF THE AHLUL-BAYT

VOLUME ONE

The Virtues of
ʿAli ibn Abi Talib

Ustadh Luqman al-Andalusi

بِسْمِ اللَّهِ الرَّحْمَنِ الرَّحِيمِ

"All the praises and thanks are due to Allah, Who has guided us to this, and never could we have found guidance, were it not that Allah had guided us!"

QURAN 7:43

Contents

I

Foreword

BY WALID LOUNÈS

I come to speak to you not as a scholar, nor as a learned man, nor as a historian. I come to you as a man with no titles. I come as a lover. And what is there not to love about the man I have come to speak of. For he is the beloved of the Beloved of Allah 🕮. He is the son of the Prophet's uncle 🕮. He is the Dweller of the City of Knowledge, nay, he is its very Gate. I come to speak to you of the one whose single strike before the enemies of Allah is worth more than the worship of all of Mankind and Jinn. What is there not to love. I have come to speak of the one whose Noble Countenance is so full of Light and Remembrance of Allah, resplendent with the Love of the Prophet 🕮, that beholding it is itself an act of worshiping Allah.

We look to him as our spiritual father, he who was born in the Ka'aba Sharifa itself. We look to him as the quencher of our thirst on the Path to Allah for he is the Spring of the Sufic Sciences, the Overpouring Vessel of Divine Secrets and Lights. We look to him as our Guiding Shaykh and Instructor of Etiquette for he is the Exemplar of Chivalry. He is the Spouse of the Best of Creation's daughter 🕮, the Father of the Ḥassanain, the Martyr, the Lion of Allāh, the Wielder of the Sword of Truth, the Keyholder of the Path, the Possessor of a Prodigious Station, the Lifelong Companion of the Beloved Prophet 🕮, and his Companion in the Next Life 🕮, Our Master, Our Star of

Guidance, Our Teacher, Sayyiduna Wa Mawlana ʿAli ibn Abi Talib ibn ʿAbd al-Muttalib ibn Hashim ibn ʿAbd Manaf ibn Qusayy ibn Kilab ibn Murra ibn Kaʾb ibn Luʾayy ibn Ghalib ibn Fahr ibn Malik ibn an-Nadr ibn Kinanah ibn Khuzaymah ibn Mudrikah ibn Ilyas ibn Mudar ibn Nizar ibn Maʾad ibn ʿAdnan.

ʿAli, the intimate companion of Muhammad ﷺ. Contemplation of his virtues illuminates our intellects and hearts. Remembrance of his qualities heightens our aspirations. Love for him and his Sanctified Family opens our chest and attracts the gaze of the Most Merciful One. Adopting his attributes grants us proximity to him and thus causes Celestial Torrents of Mercy to rush towards us. He is the Elect of Allah, the Friend of Allah, and those endowed with radiant intellects and understanding without a doubt seek to befriend the friend of the Friend.

O Allah – by the rank of Your Lion in spirit and in flesh, our Master ʿAli , enlighten and ennoble his Resplendent Countenance and grant us a portion of the Baraka and Knowledge from the Oceans of Baraka and Knowledge that You have bestowed upon him. Bless him with a blessing reserved to those who have attained Your Eternal Pleasure and Mercy, and us with him. Raise him perpetually in stations until the Day of Reckoning, and raise us with him. Have Mercy on his Noble Descendants and Forgive them, and have Mercy and Forgive us with them, and keep us in their circle until the day our Souls are called to You. Dress us in the Lights and qualities of ʿAli and adorn us with his beautiful states. Grant us a drink of his unrelenting courage in proclaiming Truth. Embellish us—O Allah—with his majesty before falsehood and his Mercy before the believers. Ornament our hearts with his love and love of his Family and grant us to cross the Veil with that love firmly rooted in our hearts, by the rank of La Ilaha Illa Allah, and may the utterance of the latter be our last words and state. O Allah – Do not take our Souls but that You have written us amongst his sincere lovers and followers, by the rank and honor of the Pole of Creation, our Master and Guide to the Unseen, Muhammad, may Your peace and blessings shower upon him and his Sanctified Family eternally, O Most Merciful of those who are merciful.

— Lounès, In Praise of the Prophet ﷺ

Introduction

BY SAYYIDI SHAYKH MUHAMMAD
IBN YAHYA AL-NINOWI

Bismillah Ar-Rahman Ar-Rahim, wa sallallahu ala Sayyidina Muhammad wa ala aalihi wa azwajihi wa sah'bihi wa sallam

In the Name of Allah, the Most-Gracious, the Most-Merciful, Peace and Blessings of Allah be upon our master Muhammad and upon his family, wives and companions, with a perfected peace.

I was sent a copy of a compilation about the virtues (*fada'il*) of Sayyidina Ali ﷺ, by brother Luqman al-Andalusi, may Allah Ta'ala protect and grant Tawfiq to him.

I was honored to browse through some of the Ahadith collected in this compilation, and found a lot of authentic and good (*hasan*) Hadiths, wal-Hamdulillah. The field of Fada'il in general is a field that allows and requires as many narratives as possible, as it helps complete the picture in the mind of the reader.

No doubt that speaking about and spreading the Fada'il Sayyidina Ali ﷺ, is a noble and brave achievement done by noble people, students of knowledge and scholars, especially in a era like ours with intensifying sectarian hate and counter hate. In such reactions and counter reactions, there remains a consistent casualty always; the truth. The foundation of Ahlus Sunnah is based on the Qur'an and the authentic Prophetic Sunnah, which accepts authentic Ahadith without prejudice or censorship. Among such Ahadith are the Fada'il of Ahlul Bayt in general, and the Fada'il of Ali in specific, as he is the Imam and Flag of Ahlul Bayt, after Sayyidina Rasoolillah, sallallahu Ta'ala alayhi wa aalihi wa azwaajihi wa dhurriyyatihi wa sallam.

Hence, Ahlus Sunnah were distinguished by equally loving both groups; the Sahaba and Ahlul Bayt, and spreading their Fada'il and Seerah, as per the facilitation of authentic narrations. While, we don't view that either group is in and within themselves a standard of guidance, yet both are close to the Prophet, sallallahu Ta'ala alayhi wa aalihi wa azwaajihi wa dhurriyyatihi wa sallam, and we only think highly of them and praise them, and follow their model in its insistence on adhering to the Qur'an and Prophetic Sunnah. The latter is the only standard of guidance, and everyone from the Sahaba and Ahlul Bayt are obliged to adhere to the Book and authentic Sunnah.

Upon examining the biographies, lives, and acceptable narratives about Ahlul-Bayt, especially Sayyidina Ali, you will find an unequivocal embodiment of the Qur'an and Sunnah. Since Sayyidina ʿAli has the longest Suhba (companionship) of the Prophet, sallallahu Ta'ala alayhi wa aalihi wa azwaajihi wa dhurriyyatihi wa sallam, examining his Fada'il gives the reader a glimpse of the Prophetic teaching and Tarbiyah.

In fact, al-Imam al-Bukhari, rahimahu Allahu Ta'ala, narrated in his authentic collection of Hadith, a narrative where the Prophet, sallallahu Ta'ala alayhi wa aalihi wa azwaajihi wa dhurriyyatihi wa sallam, told Ali: "You are to me like Harun was to Musa, except that there is no prophet after me". This Hadith is often named the Hadith of "Manzilah" or ranking of ʿAli. It shows closeness and similarities between the Prophet sallallahu Ta'ala alayhi wa aalihi wa azwaajihi wa dhurriyyatihi wa sallam, and Ali, except in the aspect of prophecy. There isn't a greater Hadith in the virtues of Ali than this, in my view.

Then, there is the Hadith in the authentic collection of Imam Muslim, where the Prophet, sallallahu Ta'ala alayhi wa aalihi wa azwaajihi wa dhurriyyatihi wa sallam, said to Ali: "Only a Mu'min loves you, and only a hypocrite hates you".

Hence, loving Ali was what Sayyidina Abu Bakr al-Siddiqq, radiya'Allahu Ta'ala anhu, instructed us as well, as in the authentic collection of Imam al-Bukhari, where he said: "observe Muhammad in Ahli Baythihi (household)". While the only authentic Prophetic definition of Ahlul Bayt indicated the five; Ahlul Kis'a, but the scholars of Ahlus Sunnah consider the honorable wives; our mothers, and the mothers of the faithful, as also natural members of Ahlul Bayt, may Allah Ta'ala be pleased with them all.

To that effect, came the very famous two lines of poetry of the Imam of Ahlus Sunnah, the founder of the ilm of Usul, the Hafidh of Hadith, the linguist, the faqih, Naasir-u-Sunnah; Sayyidi al-Imam al-Shafi'i:

> O' household of the Prophet, if loving you means to be slandered as Rafd,
> then let the worlds witness: I am a Rafidi."

Rafd is a term firstly invented by al-Imam Zayd bin Ali bin al-Husayn bin Ali bin Abi Taleb, to describe a group who espoused the love of Ahlul Bayt with the hate of some Sahaba, Allah Ta'ala be pleased with them all. The term Rafd or Rafidi, however, was also frequently used by another deviant group who espoused the love of the Sahaba and the hate of some Ahlul-Bayt or Ahlul Kis'a specifically, who are heart of Ahlul-Bayt based on the authentic Hadith of Ummu Salamah, when she was refused entry under the Kisa', despite her great and lofty status, may Allah Ta'ala be pleased with her. Some of the latter deviant group (Nawasab, sing.: Nasibi) ascribed al-Imam al-Shafi'i, the only Arab Qurashi among the great four Mujtahid Imams- rahimahum Allahu Ta'ala-, as Rafidi or Shi'i.

Al-Shafi'i was very expressive in his unequivocal love towards the Prophetic household (Ahlul Bayt) in many other statements and poetry. Loving them is indeed a sign of Iman, and distance from is a distance from Iman itself.

I pray that Allah Ta'ala accepts this compilation as a sign of love of ʿAli by our brother Luqman, and may it become an illumination that infuses love in the hearts of believers, and may Allah Ta'ala seal our lives with the His Love, His Messenger, Ali's and Ahlul Bayt, honorable Azwaaj, and Sahaba. Was-Salamu Alaykum,

Shaykh Muhammad bin Yahya bin Muhammad
al-Husayni al-Ninowy al-Shafi'i

ATLANTA, GEORGIA
20TH OF SHA'BAN 1436

Preface

BY LUQMAN AL-ANDALUSI

Firstly, I would like to especially thank my wife Ustadha Aliyah for putting up with this student of knowledge as he took this plunge into these addicting wells of Sayyiduna ʿAli ibn Abi Talib ﷺ and the Ahlul-Kisa in general. I thank Allah for her patience and love throughout. May Allah give her the highest ranks of Jannah and permission to grant Shifa for our family members in the after-life. Amin.

I would also like to thank everyone who assisted in this becoming a reality and with Allah is every Success.

Now, as we journey to extract the Jewels of Knowledge, we begin in the Name of Allah, knowing that all Praise is for Allah and that there is no strength, nor power other than Allah. All while sending peace and blessings of Allah upon the Messenger of Allah, his family and companions.

With that said, "*Truly, my Lord is Ever-Forgiving and Infinitely-Merciful.*"[2]

"*Truly, Allah and His Angels send blessings upon the Prophet. Therefore, O you who believe! send peace and blessings on him and greet him with a perfected salutation.*"[3]

Sayyiduna ʿAli Zayn al-Abidin ibn al-Imam al-Husayn, Allah be pleased with them, said, "The distinguishing feature of Sunnis (those who follow the Sunnah) is their frequent sending of prayers upon the Messenger of Allah ﷺ."[4]

It must be explained that this is the first volume of a three volume set called the Jewels of the Ahlul-Bayt and this particular volume is dedicated to the Virtues of the Righteous Caliph, The Commander of the Believers, ʿAli ibn Abi Talib. Allah ennoble his countenance. It tells of his spiritual connection to the Prophet Muhammad ﷺ as well as going chronologically over some of greatest feats.

It will also point out some of the Virtues of Sayyidah Fatimah ؏, the daughter of the Prophet ﷺ and Imams al-Hasan and al-Husayn, Peace be upon them. They as a family are known as the people of the cloak [*Ahlul-Kisa'*] and are considered the closest family to the Prophet ﷺ.

In saying that, I, the author am in no way rejecting or denying the fact that there is scholarly dispute as to who exactly are to be considered from among the family of the Prophet ﷺ.

For example Zayd ibn Arqam ؓ was asked who the family of the Prophet ﷺ was and he said, "They are the family of ʿAli, the family of ʿAqeel, the family of Jafar and the family of ʿAbbas." Husayn said: "Are all of these forbidden to receive charity [*Sadaqah*]?" Zayd said, "Yes."[5]

The wives, of the Prophet, Allah be pleased with them[6] are also to be included within the family according to the consensus of the people of the Sunnah, who state that a wife is part of a person's family as well. The main proof for this understanding is within the verse of Allah ﷻ, "The Mercy of Allah and His Blessings be on you, O the family [of Ibrahim]."[7]

Noting the truth of the above, the inner circle or household of the Prophet are the people of the cloak [*Ahlul-Kisa'*]. They are:

1. The beloved of Allah, the Prophet Muhammad ibn ʿAbdullah ﷺ

2. Caliph ʿAli ibn Abi Talib ibn ʿAbd al-Muttalib ؓ

3.   Sayyidah Fatimah az-Zahra bint Muhammad ﷺ

4.   Sayyiduna Hasan ibn ʿAli ibn Abi Talib ﷺ

5.   Sayyiduna Husayn ibn ʿAli ibn Abi Talib ﷺ

There are a myriad of verses within the Quran, sayings of the Prophet ﷺ, the scholars [*Ulamah*] and the followers [*Tabi'*] that speak in relation to the virtues and excellence of these famous five. Peace and Blessings of Allah be upon them all.

For example Allah ﷻ says, "*Everyone who obeys Allah and the Messenger are in the company of those on whom is the Grace of Allah; from among the Prophets, the sincere ones, the witnesses, and the Righteous: Ah! what a beautiful fellowship.*"[8]

Allah ﷻ says, "*So ask the People of the Reminder [Ahl ad-Dhikr] if you do not know.*"[9]

In another verse, Allah ﷻ Commands the Messenger of Allah ﷺ to tell us, "*Say! I don't ask you for any reward, other than you having love for my closest family members and if anyone earns any good deed, then We shall give Him an increase of good. Therein.*"[10]

The close companion of the Messenger of Allah ﷺ, Anas ibn Malik ﷺ[11] said, "The good deed mentioned in verse 42:23 is the love of family of the Ahlul-Bayt [meaning in this case, specifically the Ahlul-Kisa']."

Imam Jalaluddin as-Suyuti ﷺ, confirms this when he related that ʿAbdullah ibn Abbas ﷺ said:

> "When the verse, *Say I do not ask for any reward, other than you having love for my closest kin* was revealed, I asked, 'O Messenger of Allah ﷺ who are your nearest relatives whose love has now been made obligatory for us'? The Messenger of Allah ﷺ, replied, "ʿAli, Fatimah, and their two sons [Imams al-Hasan and al-Husayn]."[12]

Imam Shafi'i ﷺ, once recited a beautiful poem in regard to the mentioning of the Ahlul-Kisa' within the verse 42:23: In it he said,

O members of the Household of the Messenger of Allah ﷺ!
Loving you is an obligation, which Allah has revealed in the Quran.

On the greatness and loftiness of your station,
  it is enough that anyone who does not invoke blessings upon you,
  then it is as if he has not invoked blessings at all

Allah Commands all of us, "*O you who believe! Fulfill your duty to Allah and fear Him. And seek the means of approach to Him [Waseelah], and strive hard in His Cause, so that you may be successful.*"[13]

Imam Shafi'i 🙏, also recited, "The family of the Prophet 🙏 is my way, And they are my means of approach [*Waseelah*] to him, I hope by them that I will be given in the next life, my account of deeds in my right hand."[14]

The Prophet 🙏 himself always called people towards the love of his family as well. For example, there is a Hadith on the authority of Imam Hasan the son of ʿAli ibn Abi Talib, Allah ennoble their countenance, who narrated that the Messenger of Allah 🙏, said, "Make the love of our Ahlul-Bayt mandatory for whoever meets Allah having love for us shall enter paradise with our intercession and By He in whose Hand is my life no deed will benefit a servant except by recognizing our right."[15]

The Prophet 🙏 also said: "The best from among you is the one who has the best attitude towards my family after me."[16] and "Whoever loves me and loves these two (al-Hasan and al-Husayn), and their father and mother (Sayyiduna ʿAli and Sayyidah Fatimah), he shall be with me in my level on the Day of Judgment." [Note: they are once again the people of the cloak [*Ahlul-Kisa'*].

We love them following the best example of Messenger of Allah, 🙏 when he advises us: "Love Allah for what He nourishes you with of His Blessings, and love me due to this love of Allah, and love my Ahlul-Bayt due to your having love of me."[17]

Sayyiduna ʿAli ibn Abi Talib 🙏 also narrated that the Messenger of Allah 🙏, said, "Whoever lends a hand to the people of my family has a reward on the day of Judgment."[18]

Caliph Abu Bakr as-Siddique 🙏 said: "Know that the way to please the Prophet 🙏, is by giving his family their due rights."[19]

ʿAbdullah ibn Abbas ☙ narrated that the Prophet ☙ said, "On the day of Judgment [*Qiyamah*] every relationship and kinship will come to an end except my relationship and kinship."[20]

There is another famous Hadith that speaks of the Ahlul-Kisa' in particular as well. This is known as the Hadith Thaqalayn and it is explained by the scholars of the Quran and Hadith, that this Hadith is regarding verse 42:23 and that it is also a Mutawattir Hadith. Meaning, the numerous chains together are so strong that it cannot be rejected. In one version of this Hadith, it has been narrated from Zayd ibn Arqam ☙ who said: The Messenger of Allah ☙ said, "Truly, I leave behind two precious things among you: the Book of Allah and my Ahlul-Bayt. Truly, these two shall never separate from each other until they come to me near the Pond [of Kawthar].'"[21]

In another Version of the Hadith, there is: "O people! I am soon going to depart from here, and although I have already told you, I repeat once more that I am leaving with you two things, namely, the Book of Allah and my descendants, that is, my Ahlul-Bayt." [It is said] Then he lifted ʿAli by the hand and said: "Truly! ʿAli is with the Quran and the Quran is with him. These two shall never separate from each other until they come to me at the Pond [of al-Kawthar]."[22]

In a Prophetic saying [*Hadith*] called the Safinah Hadith [The Hadith of the Ark], there is on the authority of Abu Dharr al-Ghifari ☙ "The similitude of my Ahlul-Bayt, is like the ark of Nuh, Peace be upon him, for the one who boards it will be saved, however the one who disregards it will be doomed."[23]

All of these narrations paint a perfect picture of the Ahlul-Bayt being that spiritual simile of Noah's Ark. This simile is important because likewise in order to follow proper Deen, one has to board the family of the Prophet's Sunnah, which is the walking example of the Sunnah of the Messenger of Allah ☙; who likewise is the walking example of the Quran.

Allah speaks of this fact in the Quran, when He says, *"Embark therein; in the Name of Allah will be its course and its anchorage. Surely, my Lord is Oft- Forgiving, Infinitely-Merciful."*

ʿAli ibn Abi Talib ﷺ himself said, "By Allah, we are for this Ummah what the ark of the Prophet Noah was to his people, and we, the Ahlul-Bayt are for this Ummah what the gate of repentance was to the Children of Israel."[24]

To become more familiar with the gate of Hitta, Allah ﷻ speaks about it in the Quran, when He says: "*And when We said: Enter this city, then eat from it a plenteous food wherever you wish, and enter the gate making obeisance, and say, forgiveness [Hitta]. We will forgive you your wrongs and give more to those who do good (to others)*."[25]

The majority opinion among Historians is that the Hitta gate is located in the Land of Canaan. The Christians agree with this view according to Numbers 33:52 in the Old Testament.

With that said, the Messenger of Allah ﷺ also told us as an Ummah about our own spiritual gate, our own place to enter to purify our souls. This place is the spiritual gate of ʿAli ibn Abi Talib ﷺ and Allah ﷻ always Knows Best. This honor was given to ʿAli by Allah ﷻ; and the friends [*Awliyah*] of Allah recognize this fact.

One only needs to look into the spiritual chains of the paths of spirituality and you will see they run straight into the gate of ʿAli. This mastery shall be explained in the latter Sections of the book, In Sha' Allah.

Much more can be said, yet brevity is the Sunnah and with Allah is the Success.

The Virtues of
Sayyiduna ʿAli ibn Abi Talib ﷺ
in Chronological Order

Virtue One

THE BIRTH OF SAYYIDUNA ʿALI IBN ABI TALIB ﷺ WITHIN THE CITY OF MECCA

As we enter into the sacred mines of the life of ʿAli ibn Abi Talib, Allah ennoble his countenance; let's begin in the Name of Allah, All-Gracious, All-Merciful.

This journey begins during the year 600 CE. It is in this same year that Sayyiduna ʿAli ﷺ was blessed to be born in the city of Mecca, within the Kaba Sharif itself.

There is a difference of opinion among the Historians as to whether Sayyiduna ʿAli ﷺ was born in the month of Muharram or the 13th of Rajab or if he was born in 600 CE or a date other than that. The majority view is however, that ʿAli ﷺ was born within the Kaba' thirty years after the year of the Elephant, three years before the marriage of the Messenger of Allah ﷺ and Khadijah bint Khuwaylid, Allah be pleased with her, and Allah Knows Best.

While I was reflecting upon the fact that Sayyiduna ʿAli ﷺ was born in the city of Mecca within the Kaba',[26] it transported me back to my days as a Christian.[27] I knew the word Bakkah from the Bible, for it is defined in many older Dictionaries as being a valley where the Prophet Ibrahim brought Hagar and Ishma'il to settle. Allah/God ﷺ

then blessed them with water, which I now know is the water from the well of Zam-Zam. They also built or reconstructed the Ka'ba and renewed it as a place of sacred pilgrimage for the believers, as was the practice even before the Prophet Ibrahim's ﷺ mission.

The connection and similarities between the two religions are very deep, because in essence we mostly believe in same things. We as Muslims, also believe in the messages of the Prophet Ibrahim, Musa, David, Solomon and Jesus ﷺ. We also believe Jesus/Esa ﷺ was a Prophet, born pure without the vehicle of a father and that he is the Messiah who will come back to help the believers. The similarities are very deep indeed.

Especially after reading in the Quran where Allah says, "*Indeed, the first House [of worship] established for mankind was that at Bakkah[28][now known as modern day Mecca]—blessed and a guidance for the worlds.*"[29]

Allah ﷻ also says, "*And remember when we made the House a resort for mankind and a sanctuary, Saying! Take you the station [Maqam] of Ibraham as a place of prayer; and we made a covenant with Abraham and Isma'il, (saying) you two purify my House [The Kaba] for those who make the circuit around it [Tawaf], and for those who prostrate*".[30]

There is also a Dua of the Prophet Ibrahim ﷺ which confirms that he was in the Valley of Bakkah [Mecca], when he supplicated: "*O our Lord! I have made some of my offspring to dwell in an uncultivated valley [Mecca] by Your Sacred House [the Kaba'] in order that they may perform prayer [Salat]. So fill some hearts among men with love towards them, and provide them with fruits so that they may give thanks.*"[31]

"*Allah has spoken the Truth, therefore follow the creed of Abraham/ Ibrahim, a man of pure faith and no idolater*".[32]

"*Do you wonder at the decree of Allah, the mercy of Allah and His blessings be on you, O the family of Ibrahim? Surely, He is All-Praiseworthy, All-Glorious*".[33]

I find it beautiful that we as Muslims to this day, travel to Mecca to perform the lesser and greater pilgrimage [*Umrah* and *Hajj*] just as all the Prophets did. We do this, right now, every second, minute, hour, day, week, month and year.

Abu Hurayrah ﷺ narrated that the Messenger of Allah ﷺ said, "From one Umrah to another is expiation for what comes in between, and an accepted pilgrimage [*Hajj Al-Mabrur*] brings no reward less than Paradise."[34]

Virtue Two

To continue, Sayyiduna ʿAli's blessed mother Fatimah bint Asad, Allah ennoble her countenance, likewise lived within Mecca and followed the religion of the Prophet Ibrahim, Peace be upon him. This is called the religion of the Hunafa, as they believed in One God even before the advent of the current message of Islam delivered by the Prophet Muhammad .

Upon the birth of Sayyiduna ʿAli , it is said his mother[35] named him Haidar or Asad after her own father. This is documented within a prophetic saying [*Hadith*] narrated in the Sahih of Imam Muslim in relation to the battle of Khaybar. In it ʿAli tells Marhab: "I am the one whose mother named him Haidar."

Fatimah bint Asad is the blessed one who after the death of ʿAbdul Muttalib, played an integral role in raising the Messenger of Allah . The Messenger of Allah loved her for this and he would always remember her even after she passed from this world. He was present at her funeral prayer and asked that the community of Muslims (*Ummah*) pray for her until the end of time.

Her husband, Abu Talib returning from a business venture, wanted to name the newborn, among other names, yet they both submitted to the blessed advice of the Messenger of Allah ﷺ and changed the name Haidar to ʿAli, meaning the exalted one or the superior one.³⁶

Abu Talib, the father of Sayyiduna ʿAli ؓ, is also a very prominent figure within History. He is the son of ʿAbdul Muttalib and Fatimah bint Amr, being a full brother of the Prophet Muhammad's father ʿAbdullah ibn Abdul Muttalib.³⁷

It is related: "Abu Talib was very fond of his younger brother ʿAbdullah. At the time when the draw was taken for sacrificing ʿAbdullah. ʿAbdul Muttalib felt obliged to fulfill his pledge to Allah and it was Abu Talib who along with his brothers went to ʿAbdul Muttalib and pleaded with him to release ʿAbdullah. Lots were drawn thrice and the name of ʿAbdullah appeared on all three occasions and Abu Talib pleaded for ʿAbdullah's life and rescued him from the knife every time."³⁸

Abu Talib was truly a great man indeed, being a leader among the Quraysh of his time and he inherited the feeding of the pilgrims [*Hujaaj*] from his father ʿAbdul Muttalib of the Banu Hashim. This made him well known, and he used his notoriety for good. He also played an important part in the life of the Messenger of Allah ﷺ, helping him in his mission to the end.

Allah ﷻ speaks of this within the Quran. This event is in relation to the year 578 CE, this being the year that the Messenger of Allah ﷺ, at about eight years of age, after the death of his grandfather ʿAbdul Mutallib, passed into the custody of Abu Talib.

Allah ﷻ reminds the Messenger of Allah ﷺ of this in the Quran, "*Did Allah not find you an orphan and give you shelter and care? And He found you journeying, and gave you guidance. And he found you in need, and made you independent.*"³⁹

It is also related: "In addition to his relation with the Prophet ﷺ, Abu Talib was even more determined to protect him after the numerous prophecies about his advent. When the Quraysh were sure that Abu Talib would continue to support the Prophet ﷺ and would never give up, they brought a young poet, who was very wealthy and beautiful and presented him to Abu Talib. They told him to take the poet as his son as he would be a good support for him in his old age. In exchange they wanted Abu Talib to surrender the Prophet 🕊, for he had created discord among the Quraysh and had rendered their intellectuals as unworthy and foolish. Abu Talib replied, "has it occurred to you that anybody would surrender his dear one so that he may be killed and take up the young one of another"?[40]

Abu Talib most certainly did his best to protect the Muslims and he was one with a lot of responsibilities. This responsibility had him traveling the trade routes to feed his family.

Many times he went to Syria and other areas to gain his income. The Messenger of Allah 🕊 would frequently accompany his uncle upon these trips and he loved him dearly.

In this regard, Imam at-Tabari notes, "Once, as Abu Talib was about to leave for a trading expedition, the Prophet Muhammad 🕊 wept and could not bear to be separated from him. To this Abu Talib responded, "By Allah I will take him with me, and we shall never part from each other."[41]

In all, Abu Talib had six children. Four sons and two daughters. Each son being ten years apart from one another, Talib, being the oldest, then Aqeel, Ja'far and ʿAli.[42] He also had two beloved daughters, Fakhitah bint Abi Talib, famously known as Umm Hani and Jumanah bint Abi Talib.

There is a difference of opinion as to the faith of Abu Talib upon his death. Some day he died without professing faith, while some say he did take Shahada before death.

The famous author of the Seerah Ibn Ishaq 🕊, said: "While dying Abu Talib's lips were in motion. Al-Abbas, Allah be pleased with him, who was at this point still a nonbeliever, put his ear to his lips and then said to the Prophet 🕊 that he was reciting the witness [Shahada] the Prophet had wanted of him."[43]

Abu Talib said: "I believe that Muhammad's faith is the best of all the religions of the Universe."[44]

Here ends the section on the birth of Sayyiduna ʿAli and the lives of the beloved parents of ʿAli ibn Abi Talib.

So much more can be said, yet brevity is the Sunnah and with Allah ﷻ is the success.

Virtue Three

605 CE

SAYYIDUNA ʿALIʾS 🕸 SPIRITUAL UPBRINGING
WITHIN THE HOUSE OF THE PROPHET 🕸 AND
SAYYIDAH KHADIJAH BINT KHUWAYLID 🕸

The year is now 605 CE and Sayyiduna ʿAli ibn Abi Talib 🕸 is a young
five years of age.

The root of Sayyiduna ʿAliʾs 🕸 success can be found within the
home of the Prophet 🕸, for he was raised in the loving care of the
Prophet 🕸 and his first wife Khadijah bint Khuwaylid 🕸 whom the
Prophet 🕸 said about, "She believed in me while the people disbelieved
in me. And she trusted in me while the people belied me. And she
helped and comforted me in person and in wealth when the people
would not. Allah provided me with children by her, and He did not
with others."[45]

This access to knowledge by way of the spiritual companionship
[*Suhbah*] within the home of the Messenger of Allah 🕸 is beyond
amazing and it is a testament to having a solid family structure to
rely upon.

It was a blessing to Sayyiduna ʿAli 🕸 to have Allah Destine the
Messenger of Allah 🕸 to return the favor of his uncle Abu Talib by

9

taking him under his wing at such a young age. Meaning, in the same way Abu Talib helped the Messenger of Allah ﷺ during his own childhood, by raising and nurturing him, the Prophet ﷺ would now likewise raise and financially support Sayyiduna ʿAli ibn Abi Talib.[46]

To this end, it is related that "the Messenger of Allah ﷺ called a meeting with his uncle al-Abbas, Allah be pleased with him, telling him he thought it would be best if he (the Prophet ﷺ) would take Sayyiduna ʿAli into his custody, with al-Abbas taking Jafar at-Tayyar. They discussed this matter with Abu Talib, and Abu Talib only asked if ʿAqeel ibn Abi Talib be left with him and they all agreed to this."[47] And thus the spiritual journey began.

Sayyiduna ʿAli ﷺ himself said: "I was still a young child and the Prophet ﷺ took me into his custody. I used to cling to him and he used to feed me, and when I grew a little older, he never found me uttering a lie, nor do I ever try and deceive people. To me he was like a guiding star and I used to follow his actions and deeds carefully. I was attached to him like a foal of camel attached to their mother. He used to place before me high values of morality, and used to advise me to follow them; every year, he would spend some days at the grotto of the Mt. Hira and I used to be with him, I was his only companion then and none else could meet him at Hira, there I used to see the light of revelation, and used to smell the fragrance of Prophet-hood. Once the Prophet ﷺ told me: "Ali! You have attained a very eminent place. You see what I see and you hear what I hear."[48]

Much more can be said, yet brevity is Sunnah and with Allah ﷻ is the Success.

Virtue Four

THE SHAHADA AND PRAYER OF
SAYYIDUNA ʿALI IBN ABI TALIB ﷺ

It is beautifully related in the Seerah of Imam ibn Hisham ﷺ, "Even before the current message of Islam, ʿAli was never under the influence of polytheism because he was under the care and supervision of the Prophet ﷺ like his own son. He emulated him in all matters."[49]

The famous Historian al-Masudi ﷺ, said: "The general consensus of opinion [ʿIjma] among the Muslim historians and theologians is that ʿAli was never a non-Muslim, nor did he pray before any pagan idols, therefore, the question of his embracing Islam [although still a minor] cannot even come into question."[50]

Imam at-Tabari ﷺ, said concerning this, "Wouldn't you think that the Prophet ﷺ, being the best of creation, could distinguish if ʿAli was ready to accept Islam or not?"[51]

Upon accepting Islam, Sayyiduna ʿAli began his journey of seeking knowledge. He would study the articles of faith as well as the prayer directly from the blessed person of the Prophet ﷺ.

Anas ibn Malik ﷺ narrated that Sayyiduna ʿAli ﷺ was one of the first to pray. There is some difference of opinion as to who literally prayed first,[52] however what we do know is this: "The advent of the Prophet ﷺ was on Monday and ʿAli performed Salat on Tuesday."[53]

Sayyiduna ʿAli ؓ would pray his prayers with the Prophet ﷺ, Sayyidah Khadijah bint Khuwaylid, Zayd ibn Haritha and others ؓ

Sayyiduna ʿAli's ؓ father Abu Talib, once saw him praying and asked him what he was doing. "He answered him by saying that he had accepted Islam and had belief that Muhammad ﷺ was the Messenger of Allah."

Abu Talib had no problem with this and actually said, "Follow him, for I see that he (the Prophet) ﷺ does good to people."

In another narration "Abu Talib went to meet the Prophet ﷺ along with his son—Jafar at-Tayyar (Jafar ibn Abi Talib). They witnessed both the Prophet ﷺ and ʿAli ؓ engaged in prayer. Abu Talib turned towards Jafar and said, ʿWhy don't you also join the Prophet ﷺ and protect him from the other side just like ʿAli does?'"[54]

Sayyiduna ʿAli's ؓ ritual prayers in fact were so spiritual, that it is said: "When the time for prayer came, ʿAli ibn Abi Talib ؓ would be visibly shaken, and the color of his face would change. It was said to him, "What is the matter with you?" He, himself said, "By Allah, there has come the time of the [Trust]: Truly, We did offer the trust [*Amanah*] to the heavens and the earth, and the mountains, but they declined to bear it and were afraid of it. But man bore it."[55]

Shaykh Ahmad ibn Ajiba al-Maliki ﷺ, explains the reality of prayer [*Salat*] when he said, "The contemplative aspect of the Salat is highlighted by the fact that it is in the prayer that the believer meets his Lord as the Prophet met Him in his Night Journey [*al-Isra wal Miraj*] He said: The Prayer is the Ascension of the believer....The idea of being face-to-face with Allah appears in numerous Hadiths, as does the idea of conversation [*Munajah*] between the servant and his Lord.... When the servant begins to accomplish prayer, Allah lifts the veil that is between the man and is face to face with him [*Wajhahu bi-Wajhihi*], and a herald then cries: If the one who converses [*al-Munaaji*] in this prayer knew with Whom he converses [*man Yunaji*], he would be annihilated....There is no doubt that the presence of prayer is the most supreme of all presences, because it is the moment of intimate conversation with Allah and the mine of pure relationship in which the flashes of Divine Light shine and His secrets are revealed."[56]

There is also a beautiful example of Sayyiduna ʿAli's selflessness even within the ritual prayer itself. This action was so blessed that Allah ﷻ acknowledged it (although He Knows everything) and made it an example for others to learn from. Allah says, "*Truly, indeed, Allah is your Protector, and so is His Messenger, and those who believe and establish prayer, and give the poor-rate while in a state of Ruku' [state of bowing down]*".[57]

Abu Dharr Al-Ghifari ؓ explaining this verse said, "One day while I was saying my prayers in the company of the Prophet ﷺ, then a beggar came to the Masjid asking for charity, but nobody gave him anything. ʿAli, while in a state of Ruku', while still in the prayer, pointed his ring-finger outward towards the beggar. The beggar approached ʿAli and removed the ring from his finger. At this occasion, the Prophet ﷺ prayed to Allah to give ʿAli ease because of his generosity. Abu Dharr ؓ continued, "By Allah, the Prophet ﷺ had not yet finished his supplication for ʿAli when the trustworthy Angel Gabriel/Jibra'il ؑ descended to the Prophet with the verse 5:55." [58]

So much more can be said, yet brevity is the Sunnah and with Allah is the Success.

Virtue Five

613 CE

SAYYIDUNA ʿALI SUPPORTED THE MESSENGER OF ALLAH DURING THE DAY OF ADMONITION (YAWM AL-INZAR)

We now enter the year 613 CE, Sayyiduna ʿAli 🏵 is 13 years of age and we the community of Muslims are being oppressed by the Quraysh and their allies within Mecca.

The message of Islam was being targeted to the point that it had to be kept secret for a time. During these times the Messenger of Allah 🏵 made Al-Arqam's house a safe house [*Ribat*] for the Companions to meet, pray and learn about Islam. His house was the perfect place as it was tucked away from the hustle and bustle of the Meccan marketplaces. This secrecy continued until Allah 🏵 revealed, "And warn your family members."[59]

Imam ibn Hisham 🏵 relates in his biography of the Prophet 🏵 [*Seerah Nabawiyyah*]:[60] "The Messenger of Allah 🏵 obeying the command of Allah, then asks ʿAli ibn Abi Talib 🏵 to gather all of the members of the tribes to the home of his uncle, Abu Talib for a dinner. Upon this occasion the Messenger of Allah 🏵 took the opportunity to speak to the members of the other tribes, including the Banu Hashim".

The Messenger of Allah ﷺ said, "O sons of Abd al-Muttalib, I swear that I do not know of anyone from among the Arabs who has brought anything better than what I have brought, for I have brought the goodness of this world and the next and Allah has ordered me to invite you to these precepts and I will befriend one of you to be my brother and my successor."

After this was announced, everyone looked around as if they did not care and they really paid no attention to it at all, other than Sayyiduna ʿAli ibn Abi Talib ؓ, who was the youngest among them. He stood up and said, "O Messenger of Allah ﷺ, I am your helper upon this path."[61]

The Messenger of Allah ﷺ then put his arm around his [ʿAli's] shoulder and said, "This brother is my [spiritual] inheritor and my successor among you.[62] Listen to his words and obey his orders."

After hearing this, a handful of the people then laughed and said to Abu Talib ,"Muhammad has ordered you to obey your son!"[63]

The famous Hadith master and lover of the Ahlul-Bayt, Imam an-Nasa'i ؒ, notes that every person who laughed at Sayyiduna ʿAli ؓ was ran through within the first few battles.

Much more can be said, yet brevity is Sunnah and with Allah ﷻ is the Success.

Virtue Six

616–619 CE

SAYYIDUNA ʿALI'S SERVICE TO THE UMMAH DURING THE BOYCOTT OF THE BANU HASHIM

Another of the Virtues of Sayyiduna ʿAli ؓ is his service to the Messenger of Allah ﷺ and the believers during the time of the Boycott of the Banu Hashim and Banu Mutallib during the years of 616-619 CE. It is during this time that Sayyiduna ʿAli ؓ stood firm in his Islam. The Banu Makhzum and Banu Abd-Shams had declared sanctions against the Muslims and this was indeed a time of hardship for the Ummah, however as Allah ﷻ says, "Most certainly, with every hardship comes ease, most definitely with every hardship comes ease."[64]

Allah ﷻ also says, "*Do the people think that they will be left to say, We believe and they will not be tested?*"[65]

Ibn Hisham ؓ, relates,

> "The boycott was so rigorously enforced at times, that in the first few months the Muslims had to eat the leaves of acacia trees and the cries of the children could be heard throughout the valley."[66]

It is also related:

> "It is nearly impossible for us to imagine the intensity and extent of the efforts which Quraysh spent in its struggle against the Prophet Muhammad ﷺ, or its perseverance during many long years of that struggle. The Quraysh threatened the Prophet Muhammad ﷺ and his relatives, especially his uncles. They ridiculed and insulted him and his message, as well as his followers. The Quraysh commissioned its poets to revile him with their sharpest wits and to direct their most caustic sting against his preaching. They inflicted injury and harm on his person and on the persons of his followers. They offered him bribes of money, of royalty and power, of all that which satisfies the most fastidious among men. They not only banished and dispersed his followers from their own country but injured them in their trade and commerce while impoverishing them. They also warned him and his followers that war with all its tragedies would befall upon them. As a last resort, they began a boycott of them designed to starve them."[67]

Ibn Hisham ﷺ and others also speak of the sanctions being carefully planned and they were even put into writing, and then a parchment was put up and sealed with three stamps, and this is when "they all swore by it, and the record was hung up in the Kaba'."[68]

It is this letter that had already been eaten up by termites or ants when the famous man of Mecca named al-Mu'tim ibn Aadi went to rip it up. It is said, that to his surprise all of the parchment was gone except for the words, In your Name, O Allah!

The beautiful example of Sayyiduna ʿAli's ﷺ blessed life within this particular struggle is that he was one of those who would attend to the sick and he also sought out food for everyone. He would meet up with those in Mecca brave enough to deliver food and goods to them. Sayyidah Khadijah bint Khuwaylid, Allah be well pleased with her, also funded this until her very last dinar was spent. The prices were inflated for them in Mecca because of the boycott and even so, she, Allah be pleased with her, still gave Sayyiduna ʿAli ﷺ all of her gold to use to feed the people. Times were still rough and everyone was tried and tested, however this made things a little easier and to Allah is the Praise.

After some time the people within Mecca started to become disturbed by the echoing cries of the valley and they decided that they could no longer stand by with blind eyes. None was more outspoken to remove these sanctions than the powerful Hisham ibn ʿAmr. Hisham is the one who went to the powerful Al-Mutim ibn Aadi and others saying to them forcefully, "Are you content that the two clans of Banu Abd Manaf should perish while you look on content with following the tribe of Quraysh? Watch, you will find that they will soon do the same thing with you!"

After hearing this, Mutim ibn Aadi and others could not find it in themselves to allow this boycott to go on any longer and after the parchment was destroyed nullifying the boycott itself, al-Mutim rode into the valley with his crew, fully armed. He is the one, as is noted in History, to bring them all back into safe-keeping in Mecca. It was a beautiful action he did indeed. al-Mutim is praised to this day for it in many poems.

To continue, the peace would be short-lived because even after the Boycott ended for, the Quraysh still put pressure on Abu Talib to stop supporting his nephew and his message.

For example, ʿAbdullah ibn ʿAbbas ﷺ said concerning this: "When Abu Talib, the uncle of the Messenger of Allah ﷺ fell sick, the elders of Quraysh, including Abu Jahl, visited him and said: "Your nephew insults our gods. Do justice to us and stop him from insulting them. If he does so then we will leave him and his God alone in return. The Messenger of Allah ﷺ kept saying, Just say "There is no deity other than Allah [La Ilaha illa Allah]." The Quraysh elders were disgusted when they heard this and when Abu Jahl would not reprimand him and they turned their backs dusting their garments, as is the practice of the Arabs when there rejecting something. They then said, "Does he want that we give up all our gods and only worship his One God? This is really an amazing thing!'

The rejection of that from the Messenger of Allah ﷺ, was to tell them, as commanded by Allah ﷻ, "Say, Indeed, my prayer, my rites of sacrifice, my living and my dying are for Allah, Lord of the worlds. No partner has He. And this I have been commanded, and I am the first [among you] of the Muslims."[69]

This leads up to the next section on the Year of Sorrow. Much more can be said, yet brevity is the Sunnah and with Allah ﷻ is the Success.

Virtue Seven

619 CE

SAYYIDUNA 'ALI'S FORTITUDE DURINGTHE YEAR OF SORROW

In the year 619 CE, both Khadijah bint Khuwaylid ☙ and Abu Talib departed from this worldly life ☙. It is for this reason the year 619 is known as the Year of Sorrow. This was one of the toughest years in the life of the Messenger of Allah ☙, having lost his beloved wife and uncle Abu Talib ['Ali's father], along with his tribal protection within Mecca. The Messenger of Allah ☙ knew full well, that after many years in Mecca it was now time to make Hijrah to Madinah. The atmosphere in Mecca had become more hostile, day after day. The news of Abu Talib's death made Abu Jahl and Abu Sufyan more rebellious than ever. So much so, they sought the help of the surrounding tribes to attack the Messenger of Allah ☙, his family and companions.

The Messenger of Allah ☙ at this time is famously known to have said, "The Quraysh would never dare treat me this way while Abu Talib was alive."

Abu Talib once told the Messenger of Allah ☙, "I swear by the Almighty, your enemy cannot even glance at you with hostility, until

I am buried beneath the soil. You reveal your message and don't fear them, may your eyes be soothed with your works."[70]

After this harsh treatment in Mecca accorded to our Prophet ﷺ by the Quraysh and others, the beloved Messenger of Allah ﷺ felt it best to first head out for the city of Ta'if to spread the message of Islam. Upon arrival, he was treated with contempt and was even stoned by the children. His patience during this trial is documented within the Seerah where after being rejected by the adults and then attacked by the children of the city, the beloved Messenger ﷺ with his boots full of blood up to his ankles, makes one of the most beautiful supplications ever:

> O Allah, I appeal to you for the weakness in my strength, and my limited power, and the treatment of contempt and humiliation from people. To you, the most Merciful of all the Merciful ones, you are the Lord of the oppressed, and you are my Lord. Under whose care are you leaving me to? To an enemy oppressing me? Or to a friend you have given control of my affair? If there is no anger from you on me I will forever be content. However, your blessing is vastly important for me I seek refuge with the glory of your light, which the heavens and earth are lit form, your anger will not befall on me, nor your displeasure descends on me. To you is the supplication until you are pleased,and there is no control or power except by you.

We also have the following account from the wife of the Messenger of Allah ﷺ, "The Angel Gabriel because of this called me saying: "Allah has heard what your people have been saying to you [in the city of Ta'if], and how they have disputed you. Allah has sent the Angel of the Mountains to you so that you may order him to do whatever you wish to these people." The Angel of the Mountains called and greeted me, and then said: "O Muhammad! Order what you wish. If you like, I will cause the two mountains to fall upon them." I said: "No, for I hope that Allah will bring forth from their progeny people who will worship Allah Alone, and none besides Him."[71]

After the Messenger of Allah ﷺ returned from his trip to Ta'if, Salim ibn Abi al-Ja'd relates the following from Jabir ibn ʿAbdullah ﷺ: "The Messenger of Allah ﷺ used to approach people at the encampment settlements of the area, saying, "Is there any man who will take me to his people? For, truly the Quraysh has forbidden me from conveying the words of my Lord.'"[72]

Jabir ؓ continued: "A man from Hamdan (Yemen) approached him. The Prophet ﷺ asked him: 'Where are you from?' He replied: "I am from Hamdan.' He said: Do your people have power?' He said: 'Yes.' Thereafter, the man began to fear that his people would get mad and reject him. He went to the Prophet ﷺ and said: 'I will return to you and inform you what happens.' The Prophet ﷺ agreed to this and in the month of Rajab of the following year, a delegation came to him from Madinah [to give the Pledges of Aqaba]."[73]

While all of this happening, the Quraysh were still plotting to take the life of the Messenger of Allah ﷺ and this leads to the next section regarding the event of Laylatul-Nabit and with Allah ﷻ is the Success.

Virtue Eight

SAYYIDUNA ʿALI RISKS HIS LIFE TO PROTECT
THE MESSENGER OF ALLAH ON THE NIGHT OF
LAYLATUN-NABIT

Allah 🕮 says, "*Nothing shall ever happen to us except what Allah has ordained for us. He is our Protector. And in Allah let the believers put their trust.*"74 - ✯

We now enter the year 622 CE. This is the year wherein Allah willed for the Messenger of Allah 🕮 to make the migration from Mecca to Madinah. At this time the Quraysh met at Dar an-Nadwa and plotted to kill the Messenger of Allah 🕮 on a night now known as Laylatun-Nabit.

Allah 🕮 says about the Quraysh of this time, "*They want to extinguish the light of Allah with their mouths, but Allah will perfect His light, although those without faith dislike it.*"75

Allah 🕮 also revealed a verse in regard to this event, "*And among men is he [Ali ibn Abi Talib] who sells himself to seek the pleasure of Allah.*"76

ʿAbdullah ibn ʿAbbas 🌸 said in relation to the above verse. "ʿAli ⚔️ sold himself that night [*Laylatun-Nabit*], when he put on the cloak of the Prophet and then slept in his place."

Imam Ibn Hisham 🌸 notes, "When the Messenger of Allah 🌸 made the intention to make the Hijrah from Mecca from Madinah, men from each major tribe of Quraysh[77] were outside of the doorstop of the Messenger of Allah 🌸, so he recited a verse from Surah Ya-Sin. "*And We have put a barrier before them, and a barrier behind them, and We have covered them up, so that they cannot see.*"[78]

Being shielded by Allah 🌸, they were able to migrate and they ended up being chased down by the tribe of Quraysh. The Messenger of Allah 🌸 and Sayyiduna Abu Bakr as-Siddique 🌸 then hid in the cave of Thawr for three days until the search for them died down. The Quraysh searched for them so hard they were able to trace their trail right up to the cave itself. However, at the entrance of the cave they saw a newly spun spider web and figured it was undisturbed. Imam Bukhari 🌸 notes in regard to this, "Abu Bakr said, 'If any of them looks down at their own feet, they will see us.'" The Prophet replied to him, thus calming him down saying, "What do you think about two companions, of whom Allah is the third?"

Ibn Hisham 🌸 also notes that after three days, the two companions found a guide and proceeded to Madinah. This is the story of how the Seerah explains the Hijrah of the beloved Messenger of Allah 🌸 and Sayyiduna Abu Bakr as-Siddique 🌸.[79]

Allah 🌸 revealed a verse in regard to the event at the cave as well. He says, "*If you [people of Quraysh] do not aid him, Allah has already aided him when those who disbelieved had driven him out [of Mecca] as one of the two, when they [i.e. the Messenger of Allah and Abu Bakr] were in the cave and he said to his companion. "Do not grieve; indeed Allah is with us." And Allah sent down His tranquility, upon him and supported him with soldiers [i.e. Angels] you did not see and made the word of those who disbelieved the lowest, while the word of Allah – that is the highest. And Allah is Exalted in Might and Wise.*"[80]

Alhamdulillah, by the will of Allah 🌸 the Hijrah to Madinah was a success and to Allah 🌸 is the Praise. Much more can be said, yet brevity is the Sunnah and with Allah 🌸 is the Success.

Virtue Nine

Now while the beloved Messenger of Allah ﷺ made his migration [*Hijrah*] with Sayyiduna Abu Bakr as-Siddique ؓ one must remember the important role Sayyiduna ʿAli ibn Abi Talib ؓ played as well. He slept in the bed of the Messenger of Allah ﷺ to safeguard their escape and he also stayed behind to return all of the belongings of the Quraysh left in the trust of the Messenger of Allah ﷺ.

Allah ﷻ speaks of this in the Quran, when He says, "*Truly! Allah commands that you should render back the trusts to those, to whom they are due; and that when you judge between men, you judge with justice. Truly, how excellent is the teaching, which He gives you! Truly, Allah is the One who Hears and Sees Everything.*"[81]

Allah ﷻ also speaks to the heart of the Messenger of Allah ﷺ to comfort him, when He says, "*We know indeed the grief which their words cause you [O Rasul Allah]: it is not you that they [the tribes] deny, but it is the verses [the Quran] of Allah that the oppressors deny.*"[82]

This verse 6:33 is in relation to the above and it shows that all of the Quraysh knew of the Messenger of Allah ﷺ to be al-Amin, the trustworthy one even before the advent of his message of Islam. They knew full well to keep their wealth with such an honest one. May Allah ﷻ bless our beloved Prophet ﷺ for being such an example of trustworthiness in life. Amin.

In this event we see the bravery of Sayyiduna ʿAli ؓ as well and how he was willing to put himself right in the line of fire and yet he was calm and collected about it. He was one of the last to make the Hijrah as well. This is amazing indeed. Sayyiduna ʿAli ؓ knew the relevance of the verse of the Quran, "The Prophet ﷺ is closer to the believers than their own selves, and his wives are their mothers."[83] and he truly believed in it and implemented his life according to it.

This leads up to Sayyiduna's Ali's own migration to Madinah and thus we enter the Section on the Hijrah of ʿAli ؓ.

Much more can be said, yet brevity is the Sunnah and with Allah ﷻ is the Success.

Virtue Ten

SAYYIDUNA ʿALI IBN ABI TALIB'S MIGRATION [HIJRAH] TO MADINAH

It is said that after returning the trusts back to the Quraysh, Sayyiduna ʿAli ﷺ left in secret to Madinah.

Accompanying him were the three famous Fatimahs. They are the daughter of the Messenger of Allah ﷺ Fatimah az-Zahra, Sayyiduna ʿAli's own mother Fatimah bint Asad and Fatimah the daughter of Hamza ibn ʿAbd al-Mutallib ﷺ. By the Grace of Allah they all were able to make the trip successfully.

Imam Bukhari ﷺ relates, "By that time, ʿAli, who had left Mecca by foot three days after the Prophet, had also arrived."

When the Messenger of Allah ﷺ entered the city of Madinah, it is as Imam Ahmad ibn Hanbal ﷺ relates: "The inhabitants of Madinah never saw a brighter day in their history. Anas ibn Malik ﷺ, a close companion of the Prophet ﷺ, said: "I was present the day he [the Prophet] entered Madinah and I have never seen a better or brighter day than the day on which he came to us in Madinah, and I was present on the day he died, and I have never seen a day worse or darker than the day on which he died."

Imam Bukhari & Muslim ﷺ also related: "Every house in Madinah wished that the Prophet ﷺ would stay with them, and some tried to lead his camel to their home. The Prophet ﷺ stopped them and said:

"Leave her, for she is under (Divine) Command." It passed many houses until it came to a halt and knelt at the land of Banu Najjar. The Prophet ﷺ did not descend until the camel had risen and gone on a little, then it turned and went back to its original place and knelt again. Upon that, the Prophet ﷺ descended from it. He was pleased with its choice, for Banu Najjar were his maternal uncles, and he also desired to honor them. When individuals from the family has were soliciting him to enter their houses, a certain Abu Ayyub stepped forward to his saddle and took it into his house. The Prophet ﷺ said: "A man goes with his saddle."[84] It is recorded that the Messenger of Allah ﷺ chose to stay in the home of the Abu Ayyub al-Ansari ﷺ.[85]

It was also in this year 622 CE, that the Messenger of Allah ﷺ established the Constitution of Madinah. In Arabic it is called the Sahifatul Madinah, and in the books of the orientalists you may see it as, "The Charter of Madinah." It is well known that the Messenger of Allah ﷺ included rights for everyone including the Muslims, Jews, Christians and others.

This is also the Constitution that led to the Brotherhood pact between the migrants [*Muhajirun*] and the helpers of Madinah [*Ansar*], and with that we now enter the section of Sayyiduna ʿAli's bond of brotherhood with the Prophet ﷺ. Much more can be said, yet brevity is the Sunnah and with Allah ﷻ is the Success.

Virtue Eleven

SAYYIDUNA ʿALI IBN ABI TALIB ﷺ
BECOMES THE SPIRITUAL BROTHER
OF THE MESSENGER OF ALLAH ﷺ

The date of the migration [*Hijrah*] to Madinah and Allah Knows Best was the 23rd of September in the year 622 CE, it is from this date, that our Muslim Hijri calendar begins.

During these times, the people of Madinah [*Ansar*] were given a spiritual brother from among the Muhajirun of Mecca.

For example, Sayyiduna Abu Bakr as-Siddique was joined with ʿUmar ibn al-Khattab, Hamza ibn Abd al-Mutalllib with Zayd ibn al-Harithah, ʿUthman ibn ʿAffan with ʿAbd al-Rahman ibn ʿAwf, Bilal ibn Rabah with Talha. The examples are many. Allah be pleased with them all.

Both the Ansar and the Muhajirun were beloved to the Messenger of Allah and Allah ﷻ speaks of this when He says, "*Allah has forgiven the Prophet ﷺ, the Muhajirin and the Ansar who followed him in the time of distress.*"[86] and "*The believers, both men and women, are allies to each other.*"[87]

Allah ﷻ also says concerning this, "*And the foremost to embrace Islam of the Muhajirun and the helpers of Madinah [Ansar] and also those who followed them exactly. Allah is well-pleased with them as they are well-pleased with Him. He has prepared for them gardens under which rivers flow.*"[88]

Anas ibn Malik ؓ narrated that the Prophet ﷺ said, "The sign of Belief is to love the Ansar, and the sign of hypocrisy is to hate the Ansar."[89]

Sayyiduna ʿAli ؓ at the time of these brotherly pacts, still had not had a brother paired with himself and so he literally came crying to the Messenger of Allah asking him why?

The Messenger of Allah ﷺ told him not to worry because he was now the brother of the Messenger of Allah ﷺ himself. This made Sayyiduna ʿAli ؓ very happy and it is one of the proofs of his excellence.

The proof for the above brotherhood is within a narration of ʿAbdullah ibn ʿUmar ؓ where he narrated: "The Messenger of Allah ﷺ made bonds of brotherhood among his Companions. So ʿAli ؓ came crying saying: "O Messenger of Allah! You have made a bond of brotherhood among your Companions, but you have not made a bond of brotherhood with me and anyone." So the Messenger of Allah ﷺ said to him: "I am your brother, in this life and the next."[90]

With this migration [*Hijrah*] and the Brotherhood Pact that followed, the Messenger of Allah ﷺ stopped the war between the Banu Aws and Banu Khazraj in Madinah and he protected the Muslims against the Quraysh and other enemies. It is in these times that Allah strengthened Islam within Madinah.

Much more could be said, yet brevity is the Sunnah and with Allah ﷻ is the Success.

Virtue Twelve

624 CE

SAYYIDUNA ʿALI IS THE HERO
OF THE BATTLE OF BADR

It is always unfortunate in life, when war comes to the door of any nation. And this is exactly what happened to the Muslims of Madinah.

To begin, let's put some context into the Battle of Badr. It occurred in the year 624 CE. The Quraysh were already terrorizing the Muslims in Mecca by killing and torturing some, looting their goods and the like. They were likewise plotting on erasing Islam from the face of the earth. It is as Allah 🕮 says, *"They try to extinguish the light of Allah, however Allah 🕮 will never allow it."*

The Messenger of Allah 🕮 being newly established in Madinah, was informed that Abu Sufyan and the Quraysh were now coming from Syria with a large caravan with a lot of goods. Hearing this, the Messenger of Allah told the Companions: "This is the same Quraysh caravan containing the property [of Mecca] that was stolen from you. Go out and sneak up on it, it may be that Allah will allow you to take this advantage to get your property back."[91]

At first, Sayyiduna ʿAli ibn Abi Talib and Zubayr ibn al-Awwam, Allah be pleased with them,[92] were sent by the Messenger of Allah ﷺ to scout the activities of the Quraysh, which they did and when they achieved their purpose they returned to the Messenger of Allah ﷺ to give their advice on the matter. After discussion with the Companions, the Messenger of Allah ﷺ then decided to march on to Badr to meet the Quraysh with an army of only 313 men.

It is related: "On reaching the neighborhood of Badr, the Prophet Muhammad ﷺ sent forward Sayyiduna ʿAli ﷺ, with a few others, to reconnoiter the rising ground above the springs. They were surprised three water-carriers of the enemy, as they were about to fill their sheepskins. One escaped to the Quraysh; the other two were captured and taken to the Muslim army. From them the Prophet Muhammad ﷺ discovered the proximity of his enemy. There were 950 men; more than threefold the number of the Muslim army. They were mounted on 700 camels and 100 horses, the horsemen all clad in mail."[93]

During the moments before the battle, al-Miqdad ibn ʿAmr ﷺ addressed the Prophet ﷺ saying: "We shall not repeat what the Children of Israel had said to the Prophet Moses ﷺ, that is, 'Go, you and your Lord, to fight while we sit here waiting.' Rather, by Allah, the One who sent you to guide us, we should say: 'Go you and your Lord to fight and we shall fight your foe on your right and on your left, in front of you and behind you, till the Lord grants you victory.' Hearing this speech of Miqdad, the Prophet ﷺ smiled and blessed him. Now the Prophet ﷺ turned to the Ansar to see what they had to say. They formed the majority of his fighting force. He was apprehensive lest they should say that they had pledged to assist him only in repulsing any attack against their city, Madinah. However, Saʾd ibn Muʾadh ﷺ stood up on behalf of the Ansar and said to him that they had received him as the Prophet of Allah and had sworn allegiance to him, promising to obey him. They, therefore, were all ready to follow him, to do whatever pleased him, though it were to throw themselves into the sea. The Prophet ﷺ appreciated this statement and made it known to everyone that he had decided to face the Meccan forces, assuring them of victory.

In another report there is from Jarir ibn ʿAbdullah ﷺ who reported: "We were sitting in the presence of the Messenger of Allah ﷺ

when he looked at the moon on the night of Badr.[94] He said, "As for you all, you will see your Lord just as you are seeing this moon and you will not be harmed by His vision, so if you are capable then do not let yourselves be overcome by prayer before the rising of the sun and its setting," meaning the midday and dawn prayers. Then Jarir recited the verse, "*Glorify your Lord with praises before the rising of the sun and its setting.*"[95]

Imam at-Tabari ☁, comments about the Battle of Badr, "After the Messenger of Allah ☙ sent his men to take the caravan, Abu Sufyan learned of his plans: When he got near the Hijaz area, Abu Sufyan went about seeking news and questioning every rider in his anxiety, until he got news from some riders that the Prophet Muhammad ☙ had called out his companions against him and his caravan. Abu Sufyan even tried to avoid the battle by changing his route and calling for help. The Meccans then sent out a larger force of about 900 men to rescue the caravan. The Messenger of Allah himself was amused by this and he said, "Look at the Quraysh, they have only come out to protect their horsemen. (caravan)""[96]

Sayyiduna ʿAli ibn Abi Talib ☙ said: "When the fighting grew intense on the day of [the Battle of] Badr we sought shelter by drawing closer to the Messenger of Allah ☙, who was one of the strongest of men, and nobody was closer [in proximity] to those without faith than him."[97]

In the book al-Maghazi it is related, "It was in this Battle of Badr that ʿAli ☙ first distinguished himself as a warrior. This happened because he defeated the Umayyad champion Walid ibn Utba as well as twenty other Meccan soldiers.[98]

Phillip Hittin in his book the History of the Arabs said, "His sabre Dhul-Fiqar, which was wielded by the Prophet on the battlefield of Badr, has been immortalized in the words of this verse found engraved in many medieval Arab records, "no sword can match Dhul-Fiqar, and there is no young warrior who can compare to ʿAli."[99]

It is also related that, "ʿAli ibn Abi Talib ☙ was the standard-bearer of the Prophet ☙ in the Battle of Badr."[100]

This is the famous Battle where the Messenger of Allah ﷺ also gave Sayyiduna ʿAli ؓ his sword Dhul-Fiqar.

In the Sunan of Imam Abu Dawud ؒ, he reports Sayyiduna ʿAli ibn Abi Talib ؓ as saying: (At the Battle of Badr) Utbah ibn Rabi'ah came forward followed by his son and his brother and cried out: "Which of you shall challenge us in a traditional 3 champions' combat duel?" Some young men of the Helpers responded to his call. Utbah asked them: "Who are you?" They told him they were some young men from the Ansar. He responded: "You are brave indeed. However, we expect to face our peers, our equals, your allies from Quraysh who have betrayed us!" Hamza ibn Abdul-Muttalib took out his sword and summoned two of us to join him, me and Ubaydah ibn al-Harith. Hamza ؓ headed straight towards Utbah and after few blows, Utbah was lying on the ground.[101]

These are events that even resonate within the hearts of non-Muslims and they appreciate the struggle we gave for our freedom. For example there is within a book the Great ʿArab Conquests: "ʿAli ibn Abi Talib ؓ pressed on undismayed into the enemy ranks – it was Badr again; the Muslims were invincible.[102]

The following verses were also revealed in regard to the Battle of Badr and they are:

"Just as your Lord caused you (O Muhammad!) to go forth from your house with the truth, though a party of the believers were averse thereto; they disputed with you about the truth after it had become clear, (and they went forth) as if they were being driven to death while they looked (at it). And when Allah promised you one of the two parties that it shall be yours, and you loved that the one not armed should be yours, and Allah desired to manifest the truth of what was true by His words and to cut off the root of the unbelievers, so that He may manifest the truth of what was true and show the falsehood of what was false, even though the guilty ones disliked it."[103]

"And Allah has already made you victorious at Badr, when you were a weak little force. So fear Allah much abstain from all kinds of sins and evil deeds which He has forbidden and love Allah much, perform all kinds of good deeds which He has ordained that you may be grateful."[104]

To end, the Muslim soldiers were not savages within this battle either, as some may try and depict, and a main example of their good treatment and fairness can be seen in the narration of Abu Aziz, the brother of Mus'ab ibn Umayr ⚔, who reported: "I was among the prisoners of war on the day of Badr. The Messenger of Allah ﷺ said, "I enjoin you to treat the captives well." After I accepted Islam, I was among the Ansar and when the time of lunch or dinner arrived, I would feed the prisoners dates for I had been fed bread due to the command of the Prophet ﷺ."[105]

Alhamdulillah, it was only some months after this Battle that Sayyiduna ʿAli was to marry Sayyidah Fatimah ⚔, the daughter of the Messenger of Allah ﷺ.

Much more can be said, yet brevity is the Sunnah and with Allah ﷻ is the success.

Virtue Thirteen

623 CE

SAYYIDUNA ʿALI IS MARRIED TO SAYYIDAH FATIMAH THE DAUGHTER OF THE PROPHET MUHAMMAD ﷺ

To continue along this journey, it would be foolish not to mention that one of the Virtues of Sayyiduna ʿAli ibn Abi Talib ؓ is his marriage and companionship to Sayyidah Fatimah az-Zahra ؓ, the daughter of the Messenger of Allah ﷺ. Key figures among the Companions ؓ were involved in making this beautiful marriage come into fruition. This was a huge event within the community, for everyone loved Sayyidah Fatimah, Allah ennoble her countenance.

The Messenger of Allah ﷺ loved his daughter so much that he said, "Fatimah is a part of me, and he who makes her angry, makes me angry."[106]

She is the leader of the women of Paradise and may Allah ﷻ send His Divine Peace upon her. Amin. It is as Hudayfah ؓ narrated, "Fatimah is the chief of the women of Paradise, and Al-Hasan and Al-Husayn are the chiefs of the youths of the people of Paradise.'"[107]

The Messenger of Allah ﷺ also said, "An Angel descended from the heaven, and asked permission of Allah to greet me with peace, (he) didn't descended before, and he rejoiced me that Fatimah is the leader of the women of Paradise."[108]

This is the blessed soul Sayyiduna ʿAli ibn Abi Talib ☀, married. He was very excited about this as well. Many of the other Sahaba had offered themselves as prospects in marriage for Fatimah, yet the Messenger of Allah ☀ refused ever offer except ʿAli's. The Messenger of Allah ☀ was very happy for his daughter and ʿAli to be married and he said, "There would not be one sufficient for Fatimah if Allah had not created ʿAli."[109]

To continue, Sayyiduna al-Husayn ibn ʿAli narrated that ʿAli ibn Abi Talib ☀ said, "I got a she-camel as my share of the war booty on the day (of the battle) of Badr, and the Messenger of Allah ☀ gave me another she-camel. I let both of them kneel at the door of one of the Ansar, intending to carry lemongrass on them to sell it and use its price for my wedding banquet on marrying Fatimah ☀. A goldsmith from Banu Qaynuqa' was with me when we went to go see Hamza ibn Abd al-Muttalib ☀."[110]

Sayyiduna ʿAli's marriage to the beloved Fatimah az-Zahra highlights the high ranking of the Imam in the Sight of Allah ☀ and His Messenger. There is a Sahih Hadith on the authority of Anas ibn Malik ☀ who narrated that the Prophet ☀ said: "Sufficient for you among the women of mankind are: 1) Mariam bint ʿImran, 2) Khadijah bint Khuwaylid, 3) Fatimah bint Muhammad and 4) Asiyah the wife of the Pharaoh [*Firawn*]."[111]

The Prophet's ☀ beloved wife ʿAisha ☀ said concerning Fatimah ☀: "Fatimah walked in the same manner that the Prophet, walked. He used to say to her, 'Welcome, my daughter!' Then he would have her sit down on his right or his left."[112]

Now in relation to the occasion of the actual marriage, Sayyiduna ʿAli ☀ speaks of this beloved day in a Sahih Hadith: He said, "The Messenger of Allah ☀ fitted out Fatimah with a velvet dress, a water-skin and a pillow stuffed with lemon grass."[113]

The spiritual lessons embodied within this marriage are beyond comprehension and all parents should learn from it.

'Abdullah ibn 'Abbas ⬧ narrated in a Sahih Hadith that Sayyiduna 'Ali ibn Abi Talib ⬧ said: "I got married to Fatimah ⬧ and I said: 'O Messenger of Allah , may I consummate the marriage?' He said: 'Give her something as a dowry .' I said: 'I do not have anything.' He said: 'Where is your Hutami armor?' I said: 'I do have that with me.' He said: 'Then give it to her.'"[114]

It is also related that Sayyiduna 'Ali ⬧ said, "When I married Fatimah the daughter of the Messenger of Allah ⬧, we had only a sheep-skin on which we slept in the night and we ourselves fed and raised our goat during the day, because we had no servant."

This type of abstinence was instilled upon them by the Messenger of Allah ⬧ and he was the best of examples. This teaching of the Messenger of Allah ⬧ was not only via the vessel of words, yet it was also through the showing of proper actions, as is attested to in the narration of 'Abdullah ibn 'Umar ⬧ who said: "Once the Prophet ⬧ went to the house of Fatimah ⬧ but did not enter it. 'Ali ⬧ came and she told him about that. When 'All asked the Prophet ⬧ about it, he said, "I saw a decorated curtain on her door. I am not interested in worldly things." 'Ali went to Fatimah and told her about it. Fatimah said, "I am ready to dispense with it in the way he suggests." The Prophet ⬧ ordered her to send it to such needy people."[115]

There is also the story of the Tasbeeh of Sayyidah Fatimah [33, 33, 34] and how that replaced the maid requested by Sayyidah Fatimah ⬧ at a time of hardship. This was to teach the family that this life was not about ease and comfort, it was about struggle and putting others in front of one's own self. And for patiently bearing this struggle they were blessed with such a blessed friend as Sayyidah Lady Fizza ⬧. Lady Fizza was the manifestation of a reward one receives after having proper patience. She ended up being such a help for Sayyidah Fatimah and she worked for her at least every other day, helping around the house with the kids, etc. Lady Fizza ⬧ was from al-Habasha and she is revered to this day among the people of Spirituality.

The exact story is as follows. Sayyiduna 'Ali bin Abi Talib ⬧ narrated himself that "Sayyidah Fatimah ⬧ came to the Prophet ⬧ asking for a servant. He said, "May I inform you of something better than that? When you go to bed, recite "Subhan' Allah—thirty three times, "Alhamdulillah—thirty three times, and "Allahu Akbar—thirty four times. Sayyiduna ʿAli ﷺ added, "I have never failed to recite it ever since." Somebody asked, "Even on the night of the battle of Siffin?" He said, "No, even on the night of the battle of Siffin."[116] This is the same Tasbeeh Fatimah we all do after every prayer [*Salat*]. Ma Sha' Allah.

ʿAli ibn Abi Talib ﷺ and the family of the Prophet ﷺ are the perfect examples of the living Sunnah. Some examples of Hadith praising the family in general are as follows,

The Prophet ﷺ said to his daughter Fatimah ﷺ, "Allah wouldn't punish you, nor your children".[117]

The Prophet ﷺ told all of his companions, "Fatimah is part of me. He, in fact troubles me who troubles her."[118]

The mother of the believers ʿAisha ﷺ said, "I have not seen anyone superior to Fatimah other than her father ﷺ."[119]

ʿUmar ibn al-Khattab ﷺ once said, "I went to the house of Fatimah the daughter of the Messenger of Allah ﷺ [to visit her father] and said, "Oh Fatimah! I swear by Allah that I have not seen anyone who is dearer to the Messenger of Allah ﷺ than you. I swear by Allah that nobody is dearer to me than you after your father ﷺ."[120]

Sayyidah Fatimah's status is so great that ʿAisha the daughter of Sayyiduna Abu Bakr as-Siddique ﷺ narrated that the Prophet ﷺ, during his fatal illness, called his daughter Fatimah and told her a secret because of which she started weeping. Then he called her and told her another secret, and she started laughing. When I asked her about that, she replied: "The Prophet ﷺ told me that he would die because of this, his final illness, and so I wept, however then he secretly told me that from among his family, I would be the first to join him, and so I laughed."[121]

Sayyiduna ʿAli learned very well from the Messenger of Allah ﷺ and always treated his wife with the utmost respect. It is said, that Sayyiduna ʿAli ibn Abi Talib ﷺ never intentionally made Sayyidah Fatimah az-Zahra ﷺ angry in her entire life. This was the love bestowed between them that we all should learn from.

So much more can be said, yet brevity is the Sunnah and thus we enter the section on Imam al-Hasan and Imam al-Husayn the sons of ʿAli.

Virtue Fourteen

THE VIRTUES AND BLESSINGS OF THE
BIRTHS OF IMAM HASAN AND HUSAYN

"Al-Hasan and Al-Husayn are masters of the youth in paradise and their father (ʿAli) is even better than they are."[122]

"Whoever loves al-Hasan and al-Husayn loves me, and whoever hates them, hates me."[123]

From the blessed union of Sayyiduna ʿAli ibn Abi Talib ☙ and Sayyidah Fatimah ☙ they begot many children[124] including Imams al-Hasan and al-Husayn, Peace be upon them. They, in themselves are another virtue of the Imam, for as the father he raised them to be so great. They learned directly from him, what he himself learned directly from the Messenger of Allah ☙. This is one of the golden chains of Hadith and the Awliyah (friends of Allah) rely upon these narrations.

From the beginning of their lives, Sayiduna ʿAli ☙ implemented the Sunnah. For example, Ubayd Allah ibn Abi Rafi ☙ narrated that his father said: "I saw the Messenger of Allah ☙ say the Adhan in the ear of Al-Hasan the son of ʿAli—when he was born to Fatimah—the Adhan of Salat."[125]

In regard to the Sunnah of the Aqiqah of Sayyiduna ʿAli and Sayyidah Fatimah, it is related in the Muwatta of Imam Malik, Yahya related to me from Malik that he heard that there had been an Aqiqah for al-Hasan and al-Husayn, the sons of Ali ibn Abi Talib 🕮.[126]

Also, within the Muwatta, Yahya related to me from Malik on the authority of Ja'far ibn Muhammad that his father said: "Fatimah, the daughter of the Messenger of Allah weighed the hair of Hasan, Husayn, Zaynab and Umm Kulthum, and gave away its equivalent weight of silver as charity."[127]

The Messenger of Allah 🕮 even chose the name for al-Hasan and he also gave Sayyiduna al-Husayn his famous name.

Sayyiduna ʿAli bin Abi Talib 🕮 said: "I was a man who loved to battle and when al-Hasan was born I wanted to name him: "Harb"; it means: war. However, the Messenger of Allah 🕮 so named him: "al-Hasan". And when al-Husayn was born I wanted to name him: "Harb", the Prophet 🕮 named him al-Husayn."[128]

It should be noted, "The names of al-Hasan and al-Husayn were not known before this. In fact their grandfather, the Prophet Muhammad 🕮 was the one who named with them."[129]

Among the Virtues of our 2 masters there is from Abu Sa'id al-Khudri 🕮 who narrated that the Messenger of Allah 🕮 said: "Al-Hasan and Al-Husayn are the chiefs of the youth of Paradise."[130]

There is also from Sayyiduna Zayn al-Abdidin, ʿAli the son of Husayn 🕮 who narrated from his father, from his grandfather, ʿAli bin Abi Talib 🕮 that, "The Prophet 🕮 took Al-Hasan and Al-Husayn 🕮 by the hand and said: "Whoever loves me and loves these two, and their father and mother, he shall be with me within my level on the Day of Judgment."[131]

Another companion Bara' ibn Azib 🕮 narrated: "I saw the Prophet 🕮 placing Al-Hasan the son of ʿAli upon his shoulder while saying: "O Allah, I love him, so love him.""[132] and Anas ibn Malik 🕮 narrated that the Messenger of Allah 🕮 was asked: "Which of the people of your house are most beloved to you?" He said: "Al-Hasan and Al-Husayn."

Sometimes he used to say to Fatimah ﷺ as well: "Call my two sons for me so that I may smell them." And then he would hug them. Allah be pleased with them all.

There are many other verses, Ahadith and sayings of the scholars in regard to their blessed lives and they will be covered in Volume 3 of the Jewels of the Ahlul-Bayt Series. In Sha' Allah.

Much more can be said, however brevity is Sunnah and thus we enter the section on the Battle of Uhud and with Allah ﷻ is the Success.

Virtue Fifteen

625 CE

SAYYIDUNA ALI'S SERVICE
IN THE BATTLE OF UHUD

Let us now continue on this journey into the mines of knowledge. We enter into the Month of Shawwal in 625 CE. This is when the Messenger of Allah ﷺ marched to the Mountain of Uhud with his Companions.

ʿAbdullah ibn Abbas ﷺ said, "Among the virtues of ʿAli ﷺ is that he is one who stayed with the Messenger of Allah ﷺ at all times, during the Battle on the day of al-Mihras [the Battle of Uhud.]"[133]

It is within this battle that the Messenger of Allah ﷺ told everyone, "There is no sword but Dhul-Fiqar, and there is no young warrior who can compare to ʿAli."[134]

Sayyiduna ʿAli, his uncle Hamza and Abu Dujana ﷺ were among the heroes of Uhud. This is the battle where ʿAli truly distinguished himself as a true champion of Allah ﷻ. He fought fearlessly and ran through the standard bearer of the Quraysh, a man by the name of Talha ibn Abu Talha, and when it was immediately raised by another man ʿUthman ibn Abu Talha he fell at the hands of Hamza ibn Abd al-Muttalib ﷺ. It was raised again by Abu Saʾd ibn Abu Talhah.

This is where in the movie the Message[135] you here him say. "Do you pretend that your martyrs are in paradise and ours in hell? By Allah, you lie! If anyone of you truly believes such a story, let him come forward and fight with me." This challenge was accepted by ʿAli who also ran him through. The Banu Abd ad-Dar lost nine flag-bearers in total.

This is the same battle where a false rumor was spread about the Messenger of Allah ﷺ being killed. In the History books it speaks of man by the name of al-Laythi who saw the Prophet ﷺ fall in a ditch after being hit on the head, and then he went on shouting out loud "the Messenger of Allah is dead." This confused the generals and soldiers of the Muslims because the Quraysh were now shouting "we have killed Muhammad, we have killed Muhammad?" Hearing this, many fled with only a few staying to protect the Messenger of Allah ﷺ. Sayyiduna ʿAli ibn Abi Talib ؓ of course being one of them.

Allah ﷻ speaks about in the Quran, "When you ran off precipitately and did not wait for any one, and the Messenger was calling you from your rear."[136]

It has to be noted, that the Sahaba who ran at Uhud were forgiven by Allah for this, the proof being they did not know the news of the Prophet ﷺ dying to be a rumor, they took it to be literal and thus they did not flee the battlefield with the intention of fleeing from the Prophet ﷺ, and therefore cannot be charged with treason as some extremists may try to make it seem.

Another proof of this is as Allah ﷻ says, "Then He made you flee from them (your enemy), that He might test you. But surely, He forgave you, and Allah is Most Gracious to the believers."[137]

It has been reported on the authority of Anas ibn Malik ؓ that (when the enemy got the upper hand) on the day of the Battle of Uhud, the Messenger of Allah ﷺ was left with only seven men from the Ansar and two men from the Quraysh. When the enemy advanced towards him and overwhelmed him, he said: Whoso turns them away from us will attain Paradise or will be my Companion in Paradise. A man from the Ansar came forward and fought (the enemy) until he was killed. The enemy advanced and overwhelmed him again and he repeated the words: Whomever turns them away, from us will attain Paradise or will be my Companion in Paradise. A man from the Ansar came forward and fought until he was killed. This state continued until the seven Ansar were killed (one after the other).[138]

With this protection from the Sahaba, the Messenger of Allah ﷺ was able to get away from the Quraysh, It is related, "The Messenger of Allah ﷺ made for a rock on the mountain to climb it. He had become weighed down, and moreover he had put on two coats of mail so when he tried to get up he could not do so. Thus, Talha ؓ squatted beneath him and lifted him up until he settled comfortably up on it. As our beloved sit there with a bloodied face from being injured, Sayyiduna ʿAli ibn Abi Talib ؓ used the water to wash the blood from his beloved face and as he poured it over his head he said: "The wrath of Allah is fierce against him who bloodied the face of His Prophet ﷺ."[139]

It is related that Sahl ؓ was asked about the wound the Prophet ﷺ received on the Day of [the Battle of] Uhud. He said, "The face of the Messenger of Allah ﷺ was wounded and his front-tooth was broken when his helmet was smashed on his head. Fatimah ؓ, then washed the blood away while ʿAli ؓ, held [cupped] the water. When she saw that it had started to increase the bleeding, she took a mat and burned it until it became ash and then [she] applied it [to the wound to cauterize it] and the bleeding stopped."[140]

After the battle, as the Quraysh were fleeing to Mecca, Abu Sufyan had bribed a Bedouin going towards Madinah to tell the Messenger of Allah ﷺ that the Meccan were going to come back with a huge army to attack Madinah. Hearing this, Sayyiduna ʿAli ؓ said: "Allah is sufficient for us and most excellent of a Protector is He."

It is said that Sayyiduna ʿAli ibn Abi Talib ؓ led an army of only seventy warriors from among the Companions, in pursuit of Abu Sufyan right after they had just participated in the Battle of Uhud. They were responding to an arrogant comment made by Abu Sufyan, saying he would be back. ʿAli and the warriors camped out for three days on the ourskirts of the Hamra'ul-Asad region waiting on Abu Sufayn's army, but he never showed up, and thus they returned to Madinah.

Allah talks about this in the Quran, where He says, "*Those who responded to the call of Allah and the Messenger even after the wound had afflicted them, those among them who do good and guard (themselves against evil) shall have a great reward. Those to whom the people said: Surely men have gathered against you; therefore, fear them, but this only increased their faith, and they said: Allah is sufficient for us and most excellent Protector is He. So they returned with favor from Allah and (His) grace; no evil touched them, and they followed the pleasure of Allah, and Allah is the Lord of Mighty Grace."*[141]

So much more can be said, however brevity is the Sunnah and with Allah ﷻ is the Success.

Virtue Sixteen

627 CE

SAYYIDUNA ALI IBN ABI TALIB
ONE OF THE HEROES OF
THE BATTLE OF THE TRENCH

We now enter into the year 627 CE, for this is the year of the Battle of the Trench. Within the Seerah it is known that this battle was fought in self defense to defend Madinah against the Confederation of the Banu Nadir and Banu Qaynuqa and the Quraysh. They were upset at the Messenger of Allah ﷺ and his Companions ﷺ and wanted to seek revenge for being expelled from Madinah.

In response to this, the Confederate Army surrounded the Messenger of Allah ﷺ and his Companions in their attempt to take Madinah. Allah Revealed a Surah in regard to this event: Surah al-Ahzab.

The honorary member of the family of the Messenger of Allah ﷺ, a Companion by the name of Salman al-Farisi ﷺ advised the Messenger of Allah to dig a "Trench" around the city as were the customs of his own people, the Persians (al-Farisi). This was agreed upon by the Messenger of Allah ﷺ and thus the trench was dug around the city, and within History, this Battle is known as the Battle of the Trench [*Khandaq*].

Hafiz ibn Kathir ﷺ states: "The reason why the Confederates came was that a group of the leaders of the Jews of Banu Nadir, whom the Messenger of Allah ﷺ had expelled from Al-Madinah to Khaybar, including Sallam bin Abu Al-Huqayq, Sallam bin Mishkam and Kinanah bin Ar-Rabiʿ, went to Makkah where they met with the leaders of Quraysh and incited them to make war against the Prophet."[142]

Allah ﷻ says, "*When they came upon you from above you and from below you, and when the eyes turned dull, and the hearts rose up to the throats, you began to think diverse thoughts about Allah. There, the believers were tried, and they were shaken a tremendous shaking.*"[143]

With such a huge army as History tells, many of the People of Madinah, mostly hypocrites were becoming afraid for their lives and wanted to flee. Allah speaks of this in the Quran as well.[144]

In relation to the activities of the battle, there are many Hadith in the Sahih of Imam Bukhari ﷺ, and other books on the matter. For example, Sahl ibn Saʿd ﷺ narrated: "We were with the Messenger of Allah ﷺ in the Trench, and some were digging the trench while we were carrying the earth on our shoulders. The Messenger of Allah ﷺ said, "O Allah! There is no life except the life of the Hereafter, so please forgive the Emigrants [*Muhajirun*] and the helpers of Madinah [*Ansar*]."[145]

In another, there is narrated from Anas ibn Malik ﷺ "The Messenger of Allah ﷺ went out towards the trench and saw the Emigrants [*Muhajirun*] and the helpers [*Ansar*] digging the trench in the cold morning. They had no servants to do that for them. When the Prophet saw their hardship and hunger, he said, 'O Allah! The real life is the life of the Hereafter, so please forgive the helpers and the Emigrants.' They said in reply to him, 'We are those who have given the Pledge of allegiances to Muhammad to observe the struggle as long as we live.'[146]

It is in this battle Sayyiduna ʿAli ﷺ defeated the famous warrior ʿAmr Abd-Wudd.

This same ʿAmr was being hot-headed before the Battle of Khandaq, and he was taunting the Muslims. He had noted that he would defeat ʿAli easily. This got the attention of ʿAli ﷺ and he rose up, asking permission of the Messenger of Allah ﷺ to battle him. At first the Messenger of Allah ﷺ was hesitant to let a young ʿAli fight ʿAmr. However, after a few requests from Sayyiduna ʿAli on the matter, he was allowed to battle him with advice to use extreme caution. ʿAli agreed upon this and as he battled ʿAmr and the dust settled, it was seen that Sayyiduna ʿAli defeated this great warrior, quickly and easily as if ʿAmr was a rookie in battle. This amazed everyone around and the Muslims all shouted as if in one voice, "Allahu Akbar!" This stirred the Confederates, yet even after this they kept trying to jump or cross the trench and each time they were defeated. The Confederates continued the attack against the city of Madinah for twenty-four or twenty-seven long days ending in March of 627 CE.

One of the most beautiful happenings within this event, is the fact that with Allah ﷻ was the ultimate victory. He is the One who sent a severe storm against the invading army. This account is within the Quran. Allah ﷻ says, *"O you who believe! Remember the bounty of Allah unto you when came upon you the hosts, so We sent against them a strong wind and hosts that you saw not, and Allah Sees all what you do."*[147] *"And Allah turned back the unbelievers in their rage; they did not achieve any advantage, and Allah sufficed for the believers in fighting, and Allah is Strong, Mighty."*[148]

Much more can be said, yet brevity is the Sunnah and with Allah ﷻ is the Success.

Virtue Seventeen

628 CE

SAYYIDUNA ALI'S PARTICIPATION
IN THE TREATY OF HUDAYBIYYAH

As we continue this journey, we not enter into the year 628 CE. This is the year the Messenger of Allah ﷺ and a large amount of the Companions marched peacefully towards Mecca, in an attempt to perform the Umrah (lesser pilgrimage). There is a Hadith to this effect narrated in the Sahih of Imam Bukhari, Al-Bara bin ʿAzib ﷺ narrated: When the Messenger of Allah ﷺ concluded a peace treaty with the people of Hudaybiyyah, ʿAli ibn Abi Talib ﷺ wrote the document and he mentioned in it, "Muhammad, the Messenger of Allah ." The pagans said, "Don't write: ʿMuhammad is the Messenger of Allah, for if you were a Messenger we would not fight with you." The Messenger of Allah ﷺ asked ʿAli to rub it out, but; ʿAli ﷺ said, "I will not be the person to rub it out." Thus, the Messenger of Allah ﷺ rubbed it out himself and made peace with them on the condition that the Prophet ﷺ and his companions would enter Mecca and stay there for three days, and that they would enter with their weapons within their cases [meaning, similar to sheathing a sword].[149]

In a Hadith that explains the event of the Treaty it is reported, "The Messenger of Allah ﷺ set out at the time of Al-Hudaybiyyah with several hundred of his Companions. When he reached Dhul-Hulayfah, he had the sacrificial animals garlanded and marked and resumed the state of Ihram for the lesser pilgrimage to Mecca [*Umrah*]. He then sent several men from the tribe of Khuza'ah to gather news for him and then he proceeded.

When he arrived at a village called Al-Ashtat, his advance regiment came back and said, The Quraysh have gathered their forces against you, including Al-Ahabish tribes. They are intent on fighting you, stopping you, and preventing you.' The Messenger said ﷺ, Give me your opinion, O people! Do you think we should attack the families and offspring of those who seek to prevent us from reaching the House)''.

In another narration, the Prophet ﷺ said, (Do you think we should attack the families of those who helped the Quraysh If they come to defend against us, then Allah would have diminished the pagan forces. Or we leave them to grieve!)'' In another narration, the Prophet said, (If they remain where they have gathered, they do so in grief, fatigued and depressed. If they save their families, it would be a neck that Allah the Exalted and Most Honored has cut off. Or, should we head towards the House and if anyone prevents us from reaching it we would fight them) "Abu Bakr as-Siddique ﷺ said, "O, Messenger of Allah ﷺ! You only intended to visit the House, not to kill anyone or start a war. Therefore, head towards the House and whoever stands in our way, then we will fight him." In another narration, Abu Bakr as-Siddique ﷺ said, "Allah and His Messenger know that we only came to perform ʿUmrah not to fight anyone. However, anyone who tries to prevent us from reaching the House, we will fight him."[150]

ʿUrwah ibn Masud Ath-Thaqafi praised the Companions in the treaty of Al-Hudaybiyyah when he went back to his people saying: "O my people, By Allah! I have met kings such as Caesar, Chosroes and the Negus, but I did not see a king who is respected by his Companions as the Companions of Muhammad respect him ﷺ. By Allah, if he never spat phlegm but one of his Companions would take it by hand and rubs his face and skin with it. When he commands them, they quickly respond to his command. When he performs ablution, they are about to kill one another to use the water of his ablution. When they speak before him, they lower their voices and never stare at him out of reverence.[151]

Much more can be said, yet brevity is the Sunnah and with Allah ﷻ is the Success.

Virtue Eighteen

SAYYIDUNA 'ALI'S SERVICE IN
THE BATTLE OF KHAYBAR

To continue, we enter into the battlefield within the Battle of Khaybar. The place Khaybar itself is named after an oasis north of the city of Madinah. There is a famous Hadith in relation to this battle where Sahl ibn Sa'd 🕮 narrated: "On the day (of the battle) of Khaybar the Prophet 🕮 said, "Tomorrow I will give the flag to somebody who will be given victory (by Allah) and who loves Allah and His Messenger and is loved by Allah and His Messenger." So, the people wondered all that night as to who would receive the flag and in the morning everyone hoped that he would be that person. The Messenger of Allah 🕮 asked, "Where is 'Ali?" He was told that 'Ali was suffering from eye-trouble, so he applied saliva to his eyes and invoked Allah to cure him. He at once got cured as if he had no ailment. The Prophet 🕮 gave him the flag. 'Ali 🕮 said, "Should I struggle against them till they become like us?" The Prophet 🕮 said, "Go to them patiently and calmly till you enter the land. Then, invite them to Islam, and inform them what is enjoined upon them, for, by Allah, if Allah gives guidance to somebody through you, it is better for you than possessing red camels."[152]

In this battle Sayyiduna 'Ali dueled with the famous warrior Marhab.

Before the battle Marhab advanced towards Sayyiduna ʿAli ﷺ chanting: "Khaybar knows certainly that I am Marhab, A fully armed and well-tried valorous warrior (hero) when war comes spreading its flames."

Sayyiduna ʿAli ﷺ chanted in reply: "I am the one whose mother named him Haidar, I am like a lion of the forest with a terror-striking countenance. I return my opponents attacks more more fiercely than what they come at me with. "

In the Sahih Muslim it reads: "ʿAli ﷺ struck at the head of Marhab and killed him, so the victory (capture of Khaybar) was due to him."[153]

Jabir ibn ʿAbd Allah al-Ansari ﷺ narrates: "When ʿAli went to the Prophet ﷺ with the news of the conquering of Khaybar by himself, the Prophet ﷺ said to him: "O'Ali, had it not been for some groups of my Ummah who may say about you, what the Christians say about ʿIsa, son of Maryam. I would have said (something) about you so that you would not pass before any Muslim but that he would seize the dust from the tracks of your feet demanding blessing from it. But it suffices to say that you hold the same position in relation to me as Harun held in relation to Musa except that there shall, in all certainty, be no prophet after me."[154]

From the event before Khaybar it is said that a miracle came about. "Sayyiduna ʿAli used to put on warm clothes in summer and light clothes in winter. Upon asking why he would do so, he replied that when the Messenger of Allah ﷺ applied his blessed saliva into my eyes through his mouth, he also prayed for me: "O Allah, may ʿAli not feel hot and cold weather! Since then neither do I feel cold nor hot."[155]

Abu Rafi' ﷺ said: "We went out with Ali ibn Abi Talib ﷺ when the Messenger of Allah ﷺ, dispatched him with his flag against Khaybar. When he reached near the fortress, its people came out against him and he engaged them in battle. One of the Jews struck at him and knocked his shield from his hands. ʿAli then grasped the door of the fortress, which was made from iron and used it as a shield. It remained in his hand as he fought the Jews until Allah conquered the fortress by his hands. After Caliph Ali had conquered Khaybar he threw the door a distance of eighty feet behind his back."[156]

Ibn Ishaq ﷺ, in his Seerah says that this is because Marhab had hit the shield out of ʿAli's hand and knocked it out and thus ʿAli had to snatch the door of the fortress from its hinges.

Imam as-Suyuti ﷺ, says it took 40 men to move the door, while Imam al-Bayhaqi ﷺ, related that after ʿAli ﷺ tossed the door it took 70 men to return the door to its hinges. It was seen as a miracle from Allah ﷺ and from this point on, people really started revering Sayyiduna ʿAli ibn Abi Talib ﷺ.

Shaykh Ahmad ibn Hajr al-Haytami ﷺ, relates that ʿAli ﷺ said: "I did not snatch the door of Khaybar from its place by bodily power, but by power from the Divine."[157]

In the Mathnawi of Imam Jalaluddin ar-Rumi ﷺ, we find a beautiful story concerning the same battle, where Imam Jalaluddin ﷺ, says, "Learn how to act sincerely from ʿAli: know that the Lion of Allah was purged of deceit. In fighting against those without faith, he got the upper hand of a certain knight, and quickly drew a sword and made haste to slay him. He spat on the face of ʿAli, the pride of every prophet and every saint; He spat on the countenance before which the face of the moon bows low in the place of worship. ʿAli at once threw his sword away and relaxed (his efforts) in fighting him. That champion was astounded by this act and by his showing forgiveness and mercy without occasion. He said, You lifted your keen sword against me: why have you flung it aside and spared me? What did you see that was better than combat with me, so that you have become slack in hunting me down?[158]

The Imam goes on to say, "If the knight during the battle of Khaybar, who spat in the face of ʿAli represents the beginning of the spiritual path, then ʿAli represents the end of it for forgiving him."

Shaykh Abu Bakr Siraj ad-Din ﷺ,[159] comments on this beautiful story, when he says, "The dark night of the soul covered over is illumined by the light coming from the moon, but the moon gives off light precisely because it is not in the dark of night, but is in the presence of the solar rays, the rays of the Divine Intellect, which it reflects to those who have not yet achieved vision of the Divine sun. The knight admits as much (after spitting in the face of Ali ﷺ and being forgiven), when he speaks of the moon showing the way without speech. Sayyiduna ʿAli's unexpected sparing of his life opened the inner eye (of the knight) just enough so that he could see the moon of ʿAli's face shining upon him, inciting him to ask ʿAli what he had seen, just as one who has seen the moon but not the sun would wonder what the source of that magnificent light could be."[160]

It is as Gibbon says in his the Decline and Fall of the Roman Empire, "The zeal and virtue of ʿAli were never outstripped by any recent proselyte. He united the qualifications of a poet, a soldier and a saint; his wisdom still breathes in a collection of moral and religious sayings; and every antagonist, in the combats of the tongue or of the sword, was subdued by his eloquence and valour. From the first hour of his mission to the last rites of his funeral, the Messenger was never forsaken by a generous friend, whom he delighted to name his brother, his vicegerent, and the faithful Aaron of a second Moses."[161]

In 629 CE the first Umrah of the Muslims occurred. This was followed by birth of Zainab bint ʿAli ☙, the breaking of the treaty of Hudaybiyah by the Quraysh, the Opening of Mecca, in 630 CE the Battle of Hunayn, Taif, Tabuk and others. All of which Sayyiduna ʿAli served in, except the Battle of Tabuk 630 CE

The first pilgrimage is known as the Umrah Dhu'l-Qada'[162] and it is called such because it was the first pilgrimage of the Prophet ☙ back to Mecca after establishing a state in the city of Madinah. Shortly after the Treaty of Hudaybiyyah, the Muslims stayed for 3 days in Mecca to worship Allah according to the original rites of Hajj.

"The Prophet ☙ ordered his people, and the men who witnessed the Treaty of Al-Hudaybiyyah in particular, to make preparations to perform ʿUmrah (*lesser pilgrimage*). He proceeded with two thousand men besides some women and children."[163]

Sayyiduna ʿAli ☙ was also the standard bearer during the Conquest of Mecca (*Fathul Mecca*) in 630 CE and he served in the Battle of Hunayn, the Battle of Autas, the Siege of Ta'if, the operation against Banu Tayy and others.

So much more can be said, yet brevity is Sunnah and with Allah ☙ is the Success.

Virtue Nineteen

630–631 CE

SAYYIDUNA ʿALI BECOMES TO THE MESSENGER OF ALLAH AS HARUN WAS TO MUSA — THE BATTLE OF TABUK

There is a Hadith narrated by Saʿd ☙ and it speaks of the Messenger of Allah ☙ setting out for Tabuk. The Messenger of Allah ☙ then appoints Sayyiduna ʿAli ☙ as his deputy in the city. ʿAli was saddened by the fact that he had to stay behind in Madinah during the Battle and he was saying: "Do you want to leave me behind with the women and children?" The Prophet ☙ said, "Will you not be pleased that you will be to me like Aaron/Harun was to Moses/Musa?, even though there will be no prophet after me."[164]

"As this was happening, the hypocrites were spreading false rumors about Sayyiduna ʿAli ibn Abi Talib ☙ saying that he had been left behind because he was a burden to the Messenger of Allah ☙ and he wanted to relieve himself of him. After hearing these accusations, ʿAli took his weapons and set off until he caught up with the Messenger of Allah ☙ while he was camped in Jurf, saying, "O Prophet of Allah, the hypocrites allege that you have left me behind because you found me burdensome and wanted to get rid of me." He replied, "They lied. I left you behind because of who I have left behind, so go back and represent

65

me in my family and in yours. Are you not pleased, O ʿAli, that you are in the same position in relation to me as Harun was in relation to Musa except there will be no prophet after me?" ʿAli returned to Madinah and the Messenger of Allah ﷺ went on his expedition.[165]

Sayyiduna ʿAli, ؓ himself, knew that people were speaking ill of him.

He, himself said: "With regard to me, two categories of people will be ruined, namely he who loves me too much and the love takes him away from rightfulness, and he who hates[166] me too much and the hatred takes him away from rightfulness. Truly, I am not a Prophet, and there is nothing revealed to me. But, I work properly with the Book of Allah and the Sunnah of his Prophet ﷺ as much as I can. Therefore, whatever I have asked you to do in regard to obeying Allah, it is your duty to obey me whether you like it or not."[167]

When people used to complain about and even try to find fault within the law to blame ʿAli, the Messenger of Allah ﷺ would remind everyone of the knowledge of Sayyiduna ʿAli and then would say, "Do not complain about ʿAli, for he is sometimes rough for the pleasure of Allah."

Sayyiduna ʿAli ؓ himself would warn people, saying, "The Unlettered Prophet made a covenant with me, that none but a believer would love me, and none but a hypocrite would hate me."[168]

When all was said and done "the actual expedition ended without any bloodshed as the Prophet ﷺ found no evidence of any Byzantine forces in the area. A number of Arab tribes agree to pay a tribute tax in return for protection, switching their allegiance from the Byzantines to the Muslims."[169]

"Another innovation fought by ʿAli was that of the Khawarij or "Seceders," also known as Hururiyyah after the village of Hurur, near Kufa, where they set up military quarters. They were originally a group of up to twenty thousand pious worshipers and Hufaz of the Quran who were part of ʿAli's army but walked out on him after he accepted arbitration in the crisis with Muʿawiyah ibn Abi Sufyan and ʿAisha the Mother of the Believers. Their [meaning the Khawarij] strict position was on the basis of the verse "The decision rests with Allah alone." (6:57, 12:40, 12:67). ᶜ

Sayyiduna ʿAli ﷺ replies to this by saying, "A word of truth by which falsehood is sought!" He sent them the expert interpreter of the Quran among the Companions, Ibn ʿAbbas ﷺ, who recited to them the verses: "The judge is to be two men among you known for justice" (5:95) and "Appoint an arbiter from his folk and an arbiter from her folk" (4:35) then said: "Allah has thereby entrusted arbitration to men, although if He had wished to decide He would have decided. And is the sanctity of the Community of Muhammad not greater than that of a man and a woman?" Hearing this, four thousand of the Khawarij came back with him while the rest either left the field or persisted in their enmity and were killed in the battles of Nahrawan and al-Nukhayla.[170]

Here ends the section on the Battle of Tabuk. Much more can be said, yet brevity is Sunnah, and with Allah ﷺ is the success.

Virtue Twenty

631 CE

SAYYIDUNA ʿALI IBN ABI TALIB
AND HIS FAMILY ARE MENTIONED
WITHIN AYATUL MUBAHALA

Another one of the proofs of the honored rank of the Ahlul-Kisa' in general, is the verse [*Ayat*] al-Mubahala.

To give a little information on the event of Mubahala. This event happened in the year 631 CE, when the Prophet ﷺ was willing to swear by the lives of his beloved family lives during an oath of truthfulness with the Christians of Najran.

It has to be known Historically, that the People of Najran, are from the Northern Yemen region and it was the biggest center of it's time dedicated to Christian worship. They were influenced by the Axum Empire of al-Habasha [Modern Day Ethiopia] and you could say that the Christians of this area regarded their main cathedral to be as holy as we consider the Kaba' in Mecca.

Within multiple Seerah of the Prophet Muhammad ﷺ, there is a story that speaks of two men of Arabia who defiled this cathedral, before the message of the Prophet ﷺ, and thus Abraha came with

69

an army to Mecca to try and crush the Arabs of the Hijaz. Allah ﷻ speaks about this event within the Quran in Surah Feel (The Surah of the Elephant).

Now, the original capital of the Kingdom of Aksum, is in Northern al-Habasha (modern day Ethiopia). They ruled the region from about 400 B.C into the 10th century. The Aksum themselves became influenced by Roman Christianity because of Frumentius and later became an ally of the Byzantium Empire who were fighting against the Persian Empire.

It is said about the Axum Empire: "The kingdom was at its height under King Ezana, baptized as Abraha."[171] Yes, this is the same Abraha from the story of the Elephant. He was also a commander of King Kaleb of Axum against Dhu Nuwas.

In the Tarikh at-Tabari, ʿAbraha is said to have been the commander of a 100,000 strong army sent by Kaleb himself [to crush the Yemenis] after they first failed, led by ʿAriat. Abraha scared Dhu Nuwas so much he killed himself. Thus, Abraha seized power and established himself at Sana'a and then over the whole area in general. He rebelled against the general ʿAriat and killed him. Before ʿAriat died he cut Abraha on the face and this is why Abraha was called al-Asraam, "scar-face."

On another note, the Jews of Najran also traced their origin to the Tribes of al-Habasha and thus they planted themselves there as well, to benefit from the incense trade route within.

It is said: "Najran was a focal point of the Incense Route. All routes that left ancient Yemen to the north or west had to meet at Najran, where the routes branched into two general directions, the ones leading north through the Ḥijaz towards Egypt and the Levant and those leading to the northeast towards Gerrha near the Persian Gulf."[172]

Ibn Ishaq notes that these same Christians are whom the Negus ﷺ of al-Habasha come from. The exact quote is: "There are different traditions concerning the effect these early Muslims had on the ruler of Axum. The Muslim tradition is that the ruler of Axum was so impressed by these refugees [Jafar ibn Abi Talib 🐝 and others] that he became a secret convert."[173]

Imam ibn Hisham notes that when the Messenger of Allah 🐝 faced oppression from the Quraysh, he sent a small group of companions that included his beloved daughter Ruqayyah and her husband ʿUthman ibn Affan 🐝 to Axum, al-Habasha. He goes on to tell of how the Negus gave them refuge and protection and how he refused the requests of the Quraysh clan to send these refugees back to Arabia. These refugees did not return until the sixth year of the Hijrah (628), and even then many companions remained in Ethiopia, eventually settling at Negash in eastern Tigra.

All of the above was noted, because this is the influence of the Christians of Najran, who had a lot of influence themselves beginning at the turn of the 6th century and they maintained a powerful alliance with the kingdom of Aksum, al-Habasha.

When these same Christians of Najran received the letter of the Messenger of Allah 🐝 to accept Islam, they sent a delegation to the Prophet, to debate with him.

It is related within the Seerah that they asked the Messenger of Allah 🐝, "What do you have to say about Jesus the son of Maryam 🕊️? As you know, we ourselves are are Christians, yet we would love to hear and know your opinion on the matter in order to inform our people back home."

According to numerous Quranic Exegesis, these representatives of Najran were acting a little haughty and they were dressed in extravagant clothing and had a lot of gold on. They knew Uthman ibn Affan and Abdur Rahman ibn ʿAwf, and when even these two were concerned at the conduct of the people, they advised Sayyiduna ʿAli ibn Abi Talib 🕊️ to talk to them. He did so and thus, "Then, the representatives of Najran put on simple clothes and removed the rings and then came to the Prophet. The Prophet 🐝 replied to their salutation with great respect and also accepted some of the presents, they had brought with them. Before the commencement of mutual discussions the members of the deputation said that the time for their prayers had set in. The Prophet 🐝 permitted them to offer their prayers in the Masjid with their faces turned towards the east."[174]

Ibn Ishaq ﷺ said, "Muhammad bin Jafar ibn az-Zubayr said that, 'The Najran delegation came to the Messenger of Allah ﷺ in the city of Madinah, they entered his Masjid wearing robes and garments, after the Prophet ﷺ had prayed the ʿAsr prayer. They accompanied a caravan of camels led by Bani Al-Harith bin Ka'b. The Companions of the Messenger of Allah ﷺ who saw them said that they never saw a delegation like them after that again.[175]

After the prayer, they continued to ask the Messenger of Allah ﷺ for a reply to their presentation of the life of Jesus, and the Messenger of Allah ﷺ said: "As for today, I have nothing to say about him. You will have to stay until I get revelation telling me about the true nature of Jesus."

The following morning, Allah Revealed the verses: *"Surely the likeness of Jesus is with Allah as the likeness of Adam; He created him from dust, then said to him 'Be', and he was. (This is) the truth from your Lord, so be not of those who dispute."*

With this new Revelation in hand, the Messenger of Allah ﷺ recited these verses to the Najrani Christians[176] led by the Bishop of Najran himself Abdul Masih (some say he also known as Abu Haritha ibn ʿAlqamah) and they rejected them. This is when the Revelation came down: *"If anyone disputes in this matter with you, now after (full) knowledge has come to you, say: "Come! Let us gather together – our sons and your sons, our women and your women, ourselves and yourselves: Then let us earnestly pray, and invoke the curse of Allah on those who lie!"*[177]

It is related, "The time for Mubahala arrived. The Prophet ﷺ and members of the deputation of Najran had already agreed that the ceremonies of Mubahala should take place at a spot outside the city of Madinah in the desert. Out of the Muslims and many relatives of his, the Prophet ﷺ selected only four persons who were to participate in this significant event. These four persons were ʿAli bin Abi Talib, Fatimah, daughter of the Prophet, Hasan and Husayn, as among all the Muslims no purer souls could be found. He covered the distance between his house and the place fixed for Mubahala in a special manner. He stepped into the field of Mubahala when he was carrying al-Husayn ﷺ in his lap, and was holding the hand of Hasan in his own hand, and

Fatimah was following him and ʿAli bin Abi Talib was walking behind them. Before arriving at the place fixed for Mubahala he said to his companions: "Whenever I utter an invocation you should pray for its acceptance by saying Amin.'"[178]

The Christians decided not to go through with it and when the Companions saw that these talks were going nowhere, they finally told the People of Najran, "If you have already decided that you will remain in your religion and your creed regarding your companion Jesus, then conduct a treaty with the Messenger of Allah ﷺ and then go back to your land.'[179]

Hafiz ibn Kathir ﷺ has a story in his Tafsir, where he quotes Ibn Ishaq's Seerah, "When these verses came to the Messenger from Allah , thus judging between him and the People of the Book, Allah also commanded the Prophet ﷺ to call them to the Mubahalah if they still refused the truth. The Prophet ﷺ called them to the Mubahalah. "They came to the Prophet ﷺ and said, ʿO Abu Al-Qasim! We decided that we cannot do Mubahalah with you and that you remain on your religion, while we remain on our religion. However, send with us a man from your Companions ﷺ whom you are pleased with to judge between us regarding our monetary disputes, for you are acceptable to us in this regard.'"

Imam al-Bukhari ﷺ, recorded that Hudhayfah ﷺ said, "Al-ʿAqib and As-Sayyid, two leaders from Najran, came to the Messenger of Allah ﷺ seeking to invoke Allah for curses (against whoever is unjust among them), and one of them said to the other, ʿLet us not do that. By Allah, if he were truly a Prophet ﷺ and we invoke Allah for curses, we and our offspring shall never succeed afterwards.' So they said, ʿWe will give you what you asked and send a trusted man with us, just a trusted man.' The Messenger of Allah ﷺ said; "Verily, I will send a trusted man with you, a truly trustworthy man." The Companions of the Messenger of Allah ﷺ all felt eager to be that man. The Messenger said, "O Abu ʿUbaydah bin Al-Jarrah! Stand up."

When Abu ʿUbaydah ﷺ stood up, the Messenger of Allah ﷺ said, "This is the trustee of this Ummah.'"

The Christians of Najran as noted decided to forgo the debate and they signed this treaty with the Muslims.

Much more can be said, yet brevity is the Sunnah and with Allah ﷻ is the Success.

The events from 632-661 CE will not be discussed in this book. What should be known is that Caliph ʿAli ibn Abi Talib ؓ was the rightful fourth Caliph in accordance to the teachings of the Ahlus' Sunnah wal Jamat and that he is a spiritual master of the Muslims according to the people of spirituality.

Here ends the section on the Chronological Virtues of Sayyiduna ʿAli ibn Abi Talib.

Virtue Twenty-One

THE SPIRITUAL MASTERY OF
SAYYIDUNA ʿALI IBN ABI TALIB
THE SUHBA OF ʿALI AND THE PROPHET

Allah ﷻ says, "*Allah is the Protector of those who believe. He brings them out of the darkness into the light.*"[180]

This light gives each of us the chance to walk upon the straight path. This straight path is the path of the Messenger of Allah ﷺ, his family and close companions.

Allah ﷻ commands the Messenger of Allah ﷺ to tell us, "*Say: I ask of you no reward for this save that whosoever will, may choose a path unto his Lord.*"[181] and "*I only follow what is revealed to me [from the Quran].*"[182]

Allah ﷻ also says, "*And for every people is a guide.*"[183] and "*Enter houses through the proper doors: And fear Allah.*"[184] and "*If you are in dispute over any matter, refer it to Allah and the Messenger, if you truly believe in Allah and the Last Day: that is better and fairer in the end.*"[185]

The Messenger of Allah ﷺ has himself said in a Hadith. "I am the master [*Sayyid*] of the children of Adam and I say that with no pride."

75

"All Prophets, Adam and those after him, will be under my banner on the Day of Rising, and it is no boast."[186]

This obedience, being obligatory upon us as believers in general because of the command of Allah ﷻ to His Messenger ﷺ. *"Tell the people! If you love Allah then you should follow me. (Only then) will Allah love you and forgive your sins. And Allah is All-Forgiving, All-Merciful."*[187]

Allah ﷻ also says, *"O' You who believe! Obey Allah, and obey the Messenger and those who are given authority among you; and then if you ever dispute about something, then refer it to Allah and the Messenger."*[188]

Sayyiduna ʿAli's ؓ obedience to the Messenger of Allah ﷺ would indeed elevate ʿAli to become a spiritual master in his own right and he would prove time and again his love for Allah ﷻ and his Messenger ﷺ. Through his service to Islam, Allah ﷻ allowed him to reach the highest ranks in this life and the next.

"Those who believe and do good, surely they are the best of men."[189]

"And he who submits himself completely to Allah, and is a doer of good, he has surely grasped a strong handle. And with Allah rests the end of all affairs."[190]

Sayyiduna ʿAli ؓ is loved so much by Allah ﷻ, that he is mentioned many times within the Quran and Ahadith.

He is elevated so high because of his love and obedience to the Prophet ﷺ. Some of the rewards given to ʿAli by Allah are:

He is the spiritual brother of the Prophet ﷺ, his son in law, a man of chivalry, warrior-poet, grammarian, mathematician, law expert and chief judge [*Qadi*] among the Companions [*Sahaba*], etc.

These efforts allowed Sayyiduna ʿAli ؓ to become one of the greatest figures in all of world history in general; with his name known to peoples of every religion. His example is followed by many to this day.

Sayyiduna ʿAli ibn Abi Talib 🖎 reminds me of a narration within the Shifa of Qadi Iyad (*Chapter Regarding the Signs of Loving the Prophet* 🖎), where it is related: "If someone loves a person, he adores them and adores what they adore, otherwise he is not truthful to his love and is in fact a pretender."[191]

Sayyiduna ʿAli's spiritual state was so advanced due to his love for Allah and His Messenger 🖎. His faith so great because he was following that which Allah and his Messenger 🖎 taught. Allah 🖎 says, "*Say: 'If it be that your fathers, your sons, your brothers, your mates, or your kindred; the wealth that you have gained; the commerce in which you fear a decline: or the dwellings in which you delight— are dearer to you than Allah, or His Messenger, or the striving in His cause;—then wait until Allah brings about His decision: and Allah guides not the rebellious.*"[192]

The Messenger of Allah 🖎 said, "None of you will truly have faith until he loves me [the Messenger of Allah] more than his father, his children and all mankind."[193]

This is as the great Mufassir of the Quran, Imam Sahl at-Tustari 🖎, said, "Whoever fails to acknowledge the authority of the Prophet 🖎 over him in all situations without exception, and instead considers himself his own master, has not tasted the sweetness of faith, for the Prophet 🖎 has said, "None of you truly believe until I am more beloved to him than his own soul."[194]

Allah says, "*He who obeys the Messenger has obeyed Allah.*"[195]

The blessed character of the Prophet 🖎 being so beautiful indeed, it is as ʿAli ibn Abi Talib 🖎 said, "Anyone who came upon him by chance became filled with timidity towards him and those who kept company with him loved him."[196]

Allah 🖎 Commands the Believers in general to love the Prophet 🖎 in this fashion, for it is through submission to a proper spiritual master that one rectifies the self that calls toward evil.

Just as Sayyiduna ʿAli ibn Abi Talib 🖎 had the Prophet 🖎 as his teacher, we as well need to be educated under a guided teacher calling towards the proper Sunnah. There is no other way around it, for Islam is not a do it yourself way of life. It was founded upon heart to heart knowledge and that is the main path to our Lord.

Thus, as can be seen, we as Muslims take the Prophet Muhammad ﷺ as our chief spiritual master and he is whom we emulate. His actions, words and allowances are everything we need. It is as Allah ﷻ says,"*Indeed, in the Messenger of Allah is a good example [Uswatun Hasana] that has been set for the one who seeks Allah and the Last Day and thinks constantly about Allah.*"[197]

It is for this reason Sayyiduna ʿAli ؓ was known to say, "I will not forsake the Sunnah of the Prophet ﷺ for the opinion of anyone."[198]

It is also related that the Messenger of Allah ﷺ gave ʿAli some very good advice, "When every one seeks to draw close to Allah by means of some devotional act, do you [ʿAli ibn Abi Talib] seek the favor of Allah by associating with his wise and chosen servant [al-Mustafa], that you may be the first of all to arrive and to gain access to Him?"[199]

Sayyiduna ʿAli also knew full well, that to connect himself to the Messenger of Allah was the key to extracting the jewels of life.

His connection, so tight with the Prophet ﷺ that it would make him a living implementation of the verses, "And follow him, most certainly you will be happily guided." and "The best among you are those who have the best manners and character."[200]

Ya Allah! Please Allah envelop us within the good character of the Prophet ﷺ, with him as our guide, knowing that without a guide we would be in for disaster.

Ya Allah ﷻ, we ask you that you do not leave us to ourselves. Please allow us to take for ourselves the example of the Prophet ﷺ who taught his daughter Fatimah a beautiful Dua: "O Ever-Living, The Self-Subsisting! I seek assistance from You alone, courtesy of your Mercy; please rectify all my affairs and do not leave me at the mercy of my self even for the blinking of an eye."[201]

"*And those who struggle in Us, We will surely guide them to Our paths*."[202]

We must keep company with our Prophet ﷺ in order to drink from his Divine wells. We follow the one who asked for no wage from us, except that we love and give rights to his family.

Allah says, "*Follow those who ask of you no wage or who do not ask you for anything in return, and are themselves rightly guided.*"²⁰³ and "*O you who believe, fear Allah and keep company with those who are truthful.*"²⁰⁴

We must sit within his sacred Sunnah as Sayyiduna ʿAli ؏ would physically sit in his presence, in order to engulf ourselves in the flames of the Prophetic Sunnah.

It is related in the Muwatta of Imam Malik ibn Anas ؓ:"Luqman al-Hakim made his will and counseled his son, saying, "My son! Sit with the learned men and keep close to them. Allah gives life to the hearts with the light of wisdom as Allah gives life to the dead earth with the abundant rain of the sky."²⁰⁵

Imam Jafar ibn Muhammad as-Sadiq gave another famous Imam by the name of Sufyan at-Thawri ؓ some great advice. He said: "Seek advice in your affairs from those who fear Allah. The quest of knowledge is among the most exalted and difficult tasks; thus seeking advice is most important and urgent."²⁰⁶

Shaykh Abd al-Qadir al-Jaylani ؓ gives good advice when he said: "Learn this art of farming [the path of spirituality] by its farmers/experts, the friends of Allah [Awliya Allah] and do not think your opinion to be sufficient. Our Prophet says, "Seek help in every field from an expert in that field.""²⁰⁷

Allah says, "*And hold firmly to the rope of Allah, all together and do not become divided.*"²⁰⁸

Virtue Twenty-Two

THE SPIRITUAL TEACHINGS
OF THE PROPHET TO ʿALI

Now, concerning the science of the purification of the heart with a proper guide, once again it has to be noted that Sayyiduna ﷺ learned directly under the Suhbah of the Messenger of Allah ﷺ. Learning such Hadith as, "There lies within the body a piece of flesh. If it is sound, the whole body is sound; and if it is corrupted, the whole body is corrupted. Most certainly, this piece is the heart."[209]

The heart being so important, that the Prophet ﷺ also said, "Verily Allah does not look to your bodies nor to your faces but He looks to your hearts," and he pointed towards the heart with his fingers.[210]

It is for reasons such as these, that we protect the heart, for Allah ﷻ says He will give us His Love directly. The proof for this is, *"Those who believe and do good deeds, the Gracious Allah will create love in their hearts."*[211]

"And whoever faithfully believes in Allah, He guides his Heart."[212]

"For them He has written secure faith in their Hearts, and has strengthened them with the Spirit from Himself."[213]

We ask You, "O Allah! The Turner of the hearts, turn our heart towards Your obedience."[214]

To continue, the love manifested in the person of 'Ali ibn Abi Talib ﷺ to the Prophet ﷺ was returned to him as well. Their relationship what not only a teacher-student one, it was a very personal one. They were kin and well-acquainted with one another. This is why the spirituality of Sayyiduna 'Ali is based purely upon the Book of Allah and the Sunnah of the Messenger of Allah ﷺ.

There is also a story Sayyiduna 'Ali ibn Abi Talib ﷺ narrates himself: "I got sick, the Prophet ﷺ, visited me while I was lying down on the bed, the Prophet sat down beside me and covered me with his cloth, until I felt comfortable, then the Prophet ﷺ left to the Masjid for prayer. After praying the Prophet ﷺ came back and took away that cloth and said "Oh 'Ali stand up." Then I stood up. I felt within myself that I was healthy as if I never had any sickness. Then the Prophet ﷺ said "Whenever I asked something of Allah in the prayer, Allah granted it to me and I never asked anything from Allah but I asked that same thing for you."[215]

One of the fastest ways to purify the heart is to become firmly rooted in faith [iman]. This is a knowledge that travels far beyond book knowledge. Luqman al-Hakim ﷺ for example would reflect upon nature deeply and it brought him close to Allah by recognizing His Signs within creation itself.

Many of the first revelations revealed to the Prophet Muhammad ﷺ, were likewise concerning reflecting upon the natural world and the strengthening of faith [Iman].

On one occasion, the Prophet ﷺ told everyone to close all of the doors of the Masjid, except Sayyiduna 'Ali's door and it was in this time that the Prophet ﷺ taught 'Ali the proper recitation and meditation upon the witnessing of Laaaa ilaha illa Allaaah.

The Prophet ﷺ not only taught him how to pronounce it, rather he taught the inner meanings of it and how one should incorporate this belief of One God into one's life. When asked about this, the Messenger of Allah ﷺ told the Companions that he was commanded by Allah ﷻ to do so.

The Prophet ﷺ also taught Sayyiduna ʿAli ibn Abi Talib ؈ the deeper meanings of "He [Allah] is the First and the Last, the Outward and the Inward."[216]

These teachings entered the heart of Sayyiduna ʿAli and he is known to have been a master in the science of faith [Aqeedah], teaching it to many throughout his life. He once said, "If the veil were lifted my certainty would not be increased. And when I see a thing, I see Allah."

ʿAli ibn Abi Talib ؈ said, "A righteous deed is that you perform an action seeking no praise except from Allah."[217]

In regard to the blessed Tahleel itself, it is best to once in the lifetime make the intention to fulfill the following verse of the Quran. *"Know, that there is no deity to be worshiped except Allah [La ilaha illa Allah] and ask forgiveness for your sins and for the believing men and women."*[218]

In another verse Allah ﷻ says concerning the Messengers, *"And We have sent not a messenger before you but We reveal to him, There is no other deity than I, [La ilaha illa Ana], so worship Me."*[219]

That is the the true definition of Tawhid, to do things solely seeking Allah as a goal.

There is another good example within a story where a Rabbi named Hibr came to ʿAli ibn Abi Talib ؈ and said, "O! Leader of the believers, have you seen your Lord when worshiping him? ʿAli replied, 'This is not a proper question. I have not worshiped a Lord whom I could not see.' He then asked, 'How did you see Him?' ʿAli said, "This not a proper statement, Eyes cannot see Him in a witnessing process, but it is the hearts that see Him through the realities of belief."[220]

Sayyiduna ʿAli ؈ also said: "Mention what you will of the greatness of Allah, but Allah is Greater than anything you say. And mention what you will of the Fire, but it is more severe than anything you say. And mention what you will of Paradise, but it is better than anything you say."[221]

Shaykh Ahmad ibn Ajiba al-Maliki ؈, related, "Someone asked our master ʿAli ؈, "Dear cousin of the Messenger of Allah ﷺ where is our Lord? Or is He in a place?" His face changed and he remained silent for a moment. Then he said, "You are saying where is Allah? Questioning about place? Allah was before there was place, then He created time and place. He is now, as He was, before time and place." Meaning, Allah ﷻ was and there was nothing besides, Him, He is now as He was, so understand.[222]

The Prophet ﷺ also taught Sayyiduna ʿAli ibn Abi Talib ؓ that the one who lives the path must seek only Allah ﷻ and that is why the friend of Allah ﷻ will always be for the truth. Doing so, one seeks Allah ﷻ, al-Haqq for Himself. It is as Allah says. "Everything will be annihilated except Allah. His is the judgment, and to Him you will be returned."[223] and it is as the Messenger of Allah ﷺ said, "The truest word of a poet was the saying of Labeed, "Indeed everything except Allah is false".[224]

Shaykh ibn Ataʾillah al-Iskandari al-Maliki ؒ said, "The universe, the entirety of it, was darkness and it was lit up only due to the manifestation of the Truth of Allah in it."[225]

With these teachings, ʿAli became a beacon of spiritual guidance and this is why as Umm Salamah ؓ narrates: "When the Messenger of Allah ﷺ would become angry he would not to speak to anyone besides ʿAli."[226]

The Prophet ﷺ knew of his trustworthiness and potential and would encourage him by saying: "O Ali! You will show them the right path when there will be dissension among them after me."[227]

The Prophet ﷺ also said, "Whoever obeys ʿAli, obeys me, whoever obeys me, obeys Allah, whoever disobeys ʿAli disobeys me and whoever disobeys me, disobeys Allah."[228]

This right path is the path of guidance that we ask for everyday with our recitation of Surah Fatiha, when we ask Allah to Guide us to the straight path.

This straight path is the path of the Prophet Muhammad ﷺ, his family and the Companions who strove towards living a chivalrous life, the way of spiritual excellence [*Ihsan*], and "*Truly, Allah has prescribed goodness in all things.*"[229]

"Is the reward for excellence [Ihsan] other than more excellence?"[230]

"So blessed is Allah, the best of creators."[231]

This is the path of spiritual excellence [*Ihsan*] and this is why the Prophet ﷺ said on many occasions, we should attach ourselves with Sayyiduna ʿAli because he is the one who had the privilege of living in the home of the Messenger of Allah ﷺ from a very early age and on top of that he had a set time to learn each day. He said: "I had a [special] hour [in which to study] when I use to come to Prophet. If he was praying at that time, he use to say "Subhan' Allah", if not, he let me in."[232]

Sayyiduna ʿAli ؏ would at every moment be in the service [*Khidma*] of the Prophet Muhammad ﷺ, for he knew the benefit of sitting with the best of creation. Just being in the presence of the Prophet ﷺ was enough to increase anyone's faith [*Iman*]. This is part of the importance of sitting with the righteous, for they are the mediums and guides to Allah ﷻ.

Sayyiduna ʿAli ibn Abi Talib ؏ once said: "By Allah! When I wanted anything, I was granted it and when I kept silent, he [the Prophet] still would start to give to me [more]".[233]

Through this giving of increase by the Prophet ﷺ, ʿAli became a spiritual master among the Ummah in his own right.

Sayyiduna ʿAli also said ؏ "A man who desires that even the straps of his shoes are better than those of his friend enters into those mentioned in this verse: "And this is the abode of the Hereafter: We prepare it for those who do not seek high status or mischief in the land."[234]

There is a narration from both Abu Saʿid al-Khudri and Muʿadh ibn Jabal ؏ that the Messenger of Allah ﷺ that speaks of ʿAli's mastery: "O ʿAli, I have exceeded you in prophet-hood, because obviously there will be no prophet after me, however you exceed others in seven noble qualities. You are: 1) Of the first who believed in Allah, 2) the best of those who fulfill the promise made to Allah, 3) the best of those who adhere to the commandments of Allah, 4) the most equitable distributor among the people, 5) the best of those who dispense justice to the Muslims, 6) the one who has the best insight into controversial cases, (or the most learned in judgment), and 7) the most conspicuous in virtue and honor before Allah."[235]

Caliph 'Umar ibn al-Khattab ﷺ said: "'Ali, May Allah be pleased with him, possessed three rare and distinct virtues that if I myself, had even one of them, it would have been better to me than possessing red camels. They are: 1) His marriage to Fatimah, the daughter of the Prophet, 2) The fact that the Prophet ﷺ left the door of 'Ali open in the Masjid, 3) He was the standard bearer on the Day of Khaybar."[236]

'Abdullah ibn 'Umar al-Khattab ﷺ: 'Ali had three qualities, had I one of those, I, myself, would have loved it more than even possessing red camels. 1) He was married to Fatimah az-Zahra, 2) He was the holder of the flag of Khaybar and 3) He is the one who acted upon the Ayat an-Najwa."[237]

Other examples of Hadith with the Messenger of Allah ﷺ mentioning Sayyiduna 'Ali ﷺ in a virtuous way are as follows,

"We were created from the same tree, I and Ali."[238]

"There is a tree in Paradise called Tuba. Its roots are in the house of Ali, and its branch is 'Ali."[239]

"Whoever curses 'Ali curses me, and whoever curses me curses Allah."[240]

"The one who wants to live my life and die my death will attach himself to 'Ali."[241]

"Exemption from the Hell-fire comes with love for 'Ali."[242]

"'Ali is from me and I am from 'Ali.[243] and "You are of me and I am of you."[244]

Hafiz ibn Hajar al-Asqalani ﷺ, says in his explanation of the Sahih Bukhari: "That is, in lineage, relationship by marriage, in seniority (in Islam), in love and in other ways."[245]

The Prophet ﷺ also said, "The title of the believer's book is love for 'Ali."[246] and "The carrier of my flag in this life and the Hereafter is 'Ali."[247]

We can see from the above, Sayyiduna ʿAli ﷺ after studying with the Prophet ﷺ became the Mecca of knowledge in regard to the explanation of the Quran and Sunnah among the Sahaba. The mother of the believers ʿAisha ﷺ a great scholar in her own right, acknowledged his mastery of the Sunnah, for ʿAli's knowledge and wisdom within his time was profound to say the least.

ʿAli himself narrated that the Prophet ﷺ said, "I am the house of wisdom and ʿAli is its gate."[248] and there is another strong Hadith[249] I am the city of knowledge and ʿAli is its gate."[250, 251]

Umm al-Mu'minin Aisha ﷺ, the wife of the Prophet ﷺ said: "Ali is the greatest man of knowledge [Aalim] concerning the Sunnah."[252]

Jumay ibn Umayr said, "When I was a young boy, my mother and I went in to ʿAisha ﷺ. She mentioned ʿAli to ʿAisha, and she said, 'I have never seen a man that was more beloved to the messenger of Allah ﷺ than he was, nor a woman more beloved to the messenger of Allah ﷺ than his [ʿAli's] wife Fatimah. (Allah be pleased with them all)'"[253]

Shaykh Muhammad ibn Yayha an-Ninowi al-Husayni, Allah protect him and keep him safe, once said, in regard to the top ranking doors of knowledge. "Abu Bakr is the lover, Umar is the inspired, ʿUthman is the generous one and ʿAli is the gate [of knowledge]. Fatimah was the piece of Him and ʿAisha was the one who gave him peace. May Allah be pleased with them all."

Another two Jewels of Hadith showing Sayyiduna ʿAli's mastery, are recorded by Imam al-Bayhaqi in his Sunan al-Kubra, where the Messenger of Allah ﷺ says, "The one who wants to see Adam's knowledge, Nuh's piety, Ibrahim's forbearance, and Musa's worship, then let him look at ʿAli ibn Abi Talib." and "The one who wants to see Adam's knowledge, Nuh's intelligence, Yahya bin Zakariyya's abstinence, and Musa bin Imran's power, then let him look at ʿAli ibn Abi Talib ﷺ."[254]

It is so beautiful that Sayyiduna ʿAli ﷺ was compared to such greats, his persona is so famous within the circles of spirituality, that one of the Sultans of the path, Imam Junayd al-Baghdadi as-Salik ﷺ, said, "ʿAli is the Chief Sultan of all of the friends of Allah and it is based upon his principles and practices of spirituality that we rely upon."[255]

This is why for example, the Prophet ﷺ said, "No one would fulfill my words (on my behalf) except me and Ali".[256]

One of the reasons for this is that Sayyiduna ʿAli, studied, memorized and compiled the Quran with the Messenger of Allah ﷺ.

In a beautiful supplication the Prophet ﷺ said, "O ʿAli! I wish to achieve every such thing for you that I desire to acquire myself and I want to keep you away from all those things which disgust me."[257]

Much more can be said, yet brevity is the Sunnah and with Allah ﷻ is the success

Virtue Twenty-Three

SAYYIDUNA ʿALIʾS KNOWLEDGE
OF THE QURAN AND SUNNAH

It should be of no surprise to anyone why Sayyiduna ʿAli ☉ is mentioned in such a praiseworthy manner by Allah ☉ and his Messenger ☉, for he is so mentioned because he learned the Quran and Sunnah directly from the Messenger of Allah ☉, who went over the Quran with the Angel Jibraʾil ☉ who received it directly from Allah ☉. There is no other chain in regard to the Quran that is this sacred and Allah ☉ knows best.

It is reported from the mother of the believers ʿAisha that the leader of the women of Paradise Fatimah az-Zahra, Allah be pleased with them, said, "The Prophet ☉, confided to me, The Angel Jibraʾil, Peace be upon him, used to review the Quran with me every year, but this year he reviewed it with me twice. I only think that my time is approaching.'"

ʿAbdullah ibn ʿAbbas ☉ said, "The Prophet ☉ was the most generous of people, and he was at his most generous during the month of Ramadan because Jibraʾil used to met him every night in the month of Ramadan until it ended. The Messenger of Allah ☉ used to review the Quran with him. When Jibraʾil met him, he was more generous with good than the blowing wind."²⁵⁸

Now, please reflect once again on the fact that Sayyiduna ʿAli ﷺ learned the Quran directly from the Messenger of Allah ﷺ and you will see why the great scholar of the Quran, ʿAbdullah ibn Abbas ﷺ said, "The Quran has been revealed with seven readings, each with an inner meaning and an outer. ʿAli ibn Abi Talib ﷺ knows the outer [az-Zahir] and the inner [al-Baatin]." He also said, "Whatever I have taken from the Tafsir of the Quran is on the authority of ʿAli ibn Abi Talib."[259]

This is one of the reasons the Messenger of Allah ﷺ said, "'Ali is with the Quran and the Quran is with ʿAli, they will never separate until they reach me at the Pond [Fountain of Kawthar]."[260]

It is well known that even in the earliest times of Islam, Sayyiduna ʿAli ﷺ loved the Quran and he never missed a class in regard to the Quran and its meaning. These classes during the first few years of revelation were held within the House of Arqam. During these times mostly Chapters calling towards [faith] Iman and warning of the day of Judgment were being revealed.[261] Sayyiduna ʿAli and others among the Sahaba would also be given classes on Islamic Etiquette [Adab] taught directly by the words and the blessed example of the Messenger of Allah ﷺ.

Allah ﷻ says concerning the blessed example of the Prophet ﷺ, "And We have not sent you, except as a Mercy to the worlds."[262]

"Nor does he [the Prophet] speak out of his own desire. It is no less than a Revelation that is revealed."[263]

Allah ﷻ says, "And We have also sent down unto you the Dhikr [Quran], that you may explain clearly to men what is sent down to them."[264]

"And We send down of the Quran that which is healing and mercy for the believers."[265]

Bearing this in mind it is famously known that ʿAli ibn Abi Talib's love for the Quran was strong. Allah ﷻ says concerning those who love the Quran, "The People of the Quran [Ahlul-Quran] are the people of Allah [Ahlul-Lah] and His elect."[266] and He says concerning His Quran itself, "This is not fabricated Hadith; this confirms all previous *scriptures, provides the details of everything, and is a beacon and mercy for those who believe."*[267]

This communicating of the Quran and Sunnah is not a light matter at all. The Companions of the Messenger of Allah, Allah be pleased with them, would fear relaying unsound knowledge of the Quran, that ʿAbdullah ibn Masud ؓ is reported to have said: "When a man among us learned ten verses, he would not move on until he had understood their meanings and how to act by them."[268]

Imam Jalaluddin as-Suyuti ؒ, said: "The Companions, Allah be pleased with them, knew it very well that the knowledge of Islam is for practice, it is not knowledge just for the sake of knowledge. ʿAbdullah ibn ʿUmar ؓ ok eight years to learn the second Chapter of the Quran [Surah al-Baqarah]."[269]

Allah ﷻ says, *"Then do they not reflect upon the Quran? If it had been from [any] other than Allah, they would have found within it much contradiction."*[270]

Sayyiduna ʿAli ؓ would also remind his students, "There is no good in reading the Quran, if you do not ponder over it."[271]

This is because Allah ﷻ says, *"And (it is) a Quran which I have divided into parts in order that you may recite it to the people gradually, and I have revealed it by successive revelation."*[272]

Therefore, this recitation and reflection upon the Quran was a daily part of the lives of ʿAli ibn Abi Talib ؓ and all of the righteous, Allah be pleased with them. They would be afraid if they did not read the Quran, verses such as the following would be about them. Allah ﷻ says, "And be not like those who forgot Allah, so He made them forget their own souls; these it is that are the transgressors."[273]

Allah ﷻ tells us all, *"And remember that which is recited in your houses of the revelations of Allah and the Wisdom."*[274]

As was noted, these revelations would be taught by the Messenger of Allah ﷺ and he would remind the Companions to teach the Quran, based upon the verse, *"And if any one of the polytheists seeks your protection, then grant him protection so that he may hear the Words of Allah [the Quran]."*[275]

Jabir ibn ʿAbdullah 🙷 also reported that the Prophet 🙷 used to invite people to Islam during the Hajj season and would say, "Who are willing to give me asylum so that I can convey the Speech of my Lord, for the Quraysh have prevented me from conveying the Speech of my Lord."[276]

All praise is due to Allah 🙷, may Allah bless the Prophet 🙷 for his hard work. The rewards for spreading the knowledge of the Quran and Sunnah are many.

Sayyiduna ʿAli ibn Abi Talib 🙷 narrated that the Messenger of Allah 🙷 said, "The best among you are those who learn the Quran and teach it."[277]

On another occasion, Sayyiduna ʿAli 🙷 narrated that the Messenger of Allah 🙷 said, "Whoever reads the Quran and learns it by heart, and regards what it makes lawful as lawful and its unlawful as forbidden, will be admitted into Paradise by Almighty Allah Who will also accept his intercession in respect of ten such persons of his family who shall have been doomed to Hell."[278]

This knowledge of the Quran is so important, that it is Halal to envy a person who has possession it. The proof for this is within a Hadith where ʿAbdullah ibn ʿUmar 🙷 narrated that the Messenger of Allah 🙷 said, "Envy is justified, only in regard to two types of people: 1) a person whom Allah has given knowledge of the Quran, and so he recites it during the night and during the day; and 2) a person whom Allah has given wealth and so he spends from it during the night and during the day."[279]

The Sciences of the Quran, have to be beloved to the hearts of the believers. For the reality is that Quran is a personal conversation with the Lord of the worlds. Within it, lay the guidance we need as Allah says, "This is the Book; in it is guidance sure, without doubt, to those who are fearfully aware of Allah."[280]

Sayyiduna ʿAli ibn Abi Talib 🙷 was most certainly one who was fearfully aware of Allah 🙷 and it is a shame that not many know of the significant role he played in the compilation of the Quran, both during the time of the Messenger of Allah 🙷 and after his passing.

'Ali's knowledge of the Quran was so vast, that he not only compiled the Quran, he memorized it in its entirety as well. This allowed him to also play the role of a scribe of the Messenger of Allah ﷺ.

Allah says, "*It is Allah who sent to you [O' Muhammad] the Book [Quran], wherein are some decisive verses —they are the basis of the Book and others having variable meanings. Men with perversity in their hearts emphasize the unclear therein (seeking to mislead); while none knows the Quran's hidden meaning except Allah and the erudite (firmly rooted) in knowledge; who say We believe in it, all is from our Lord." Nevertheless, none heeds this save those endowed with wisdom.*" (Quran, 3:7)

As was explained, Sayyiduna 'Ali ؓ knew these verses is their totality and thus it cannot be of any surprise when 'Abdullah ibn Masud ؓ said, "Ali is with the Quran and the Quran is with 'Ali, they will never separate until they reach me at the Fountain of Kawthar."[281] and as was noted: "The Quran has been revealed with seven readings, each with an inner meaning and an outer. 'Ali ibn Abi Talib ؓ knows the outer [*az-Zahir*] and the inner [*al-Baatin*]." He also said, "Whatever I have taken from the Tafsir of the Quran is on the authority of 'Ali ibn Abi Talib."[282]

The Messenger of Allah ﷺ saw the greatness of 'Ali's vast knowledge and on another another occasion he said to him: "Truly, you shall do battle to implement the Quran, just as you have done in compiling its revelation."[283] and "You are going to be able to inform my nation about the truth. after they start disputing when I depart."[284]

'Ali ibn Abi Talib, would fulfill these prophecies, as is related "After the death of the Messenger of Allah, 'Ali ibn Abi Talib ؓ sat down in his house and said that he had sworn an oath that he would not put on his outdoor clothes or leave his house until he collected together the Quran."[285]

In relation to Sayyiduna 'Ali's compilation of the Quran, it is reported that "It is according to this transcript that Sunni scholars relate that the first Chapter of Quran which was sent down to the Prophet ﷺ was Chapter al-Iqra (al-Alaq, Chapter 96)."[286]

It is also related, "In ʿAli's Mushaf the Commander of the Faithful had specified the *Naskh*[287] and the *Mansukh*[288], however I was unable to trace it despite my extensive efforts in this regard, including the letter I wrote to Madinah."[289]

It is for this reason as ibn Saʿd ♦, said in his *Tabaqat al-Kubra*, "The Quran is the magnum opus within the life of ʿAli ♦ and it is related that ʿAli was known most specifically for his vast knowledge and of his special dedication to the Quran."[290]

Abu Nasr Abdullahi as-Sarraj ♦ relates that when Imam Junayd al-Baghdadi ♦ was asked about Sayyiduna Ali's ♦ knowledge in regard to the esoteric field, and he said, "If it were not for the fact that ʿAli ♦ had been engaged in numerous wars, the world may have benefited more from his contributions to the knowledge of esoteric things, for he was one who had been vouchsafed Divine Knowledge."[291]

These are the reasons the Messenger of Allah ♦ said, "O ʿAli! Whoever separates from me, he separates from Allah; and whoever separates from you, he separates from me."[292]

"The one who wants to live my life and die my death will attach himself to ʿAli."[293]

As was noted, Sayyiduna ʿAli ♦ himself said concerning his knowledge of the Quran,[294] "You will not ask me about any verse in the Book of Allah or about any Sunnah from the Messenger of Allah, except that I will inform you about that." and "By Allah, no verse of the Quran has been sent down without my knowing about whom or what it was revealed and where it was revealed as taught to me by the Messenger of Allah ♦. My Lord has gifted me with a mind that is quick in retaining and understanding knowledge, and a tongue which speaks eloquently."[295]

He would also say, "Ask me before you lose me. By Allah, if you ask me about anything that could happen up to the Day of Judgment, I will tell you about it. Ask me about the Book of Allah, because by Allah there is no verse that I do not know whether it was revealed during the night or the day, or whether it was revealed on a plain or on a mountain."[296]

Oh, yes! *"In this, there is indeed a Reminder for everyone who has a heart, or will give ear while he is a witness."*[297]

The people of spirituality say if you want to see the realities of the Quran and if you want to understand true belief in Allah, then you go to the understanding, life and teachings of ʿAli ibn Abi Talib ؏.

This is because as was noted in all of the above, his life is a walking example of the Sunnah, just as the Messenger of Allah ﷺ is a walking example of the Quran.

Much more can be said, yet brevity is the Sunnah and with Allah ﷻ is the Success.

Extra Benefit One

THE KNOWLEDGE AND WISDOM OF SAYYIDUNA ʿALI IBN ABI TALIB

Allah ﷻ says, "*Allah will exalt in degree those of you who believe, and those who have been granted knowledge. And Allah is Well-Acquainted with what you do.*"[298] and "*Whosoever is given wisdom, is given abundant good.*"[299]

The benefit of Sayyiduna ʿAli's ﷺ companionship with the Prophet ﷺ allowed major jewels of knowledge and wisdom to be extracted therein. This is seen in regard to the amount of knowledge and wisdom he gained from the blessed example of the Prophet.

It can be said that Sayyiduna ʿAli ﷺ because of this is considered the Mecca of knowledge in regard to the explanation of the Quran and Sunnah. The mother of the believers ʿAisha ﷺ is a great scholar in her own right, and she acknowledged his mastery of the Sunnah, for Sayyiduna ʿAli's knowledge and wisdom within his time was profound to say the least.

Each spiritual path of the Sufis flows through him. This is noted by Sayyiduna ʿAli himself who narrated that the Messenger of Allah ﷺ said, "I am the house of wisdom and ʿAli ﷺ is its gate."[300] and there is another strong Hadith[301] "I am the city of knowledge and ʿAli is its gate."[302] [303]

Some of the beloved Imam's famous sayings are, "The servant of Allah should not fear except his sins, and should not hope except in his Lord. The ignorant should not be ashamed to ask, and the knowledgeable should not be ashamed to say – if he does not know something – 'Allah knows best.' Patience to faith is like the head to the rest of the body: if the head is cut off, the body will rot. And one who has no patience, has no faith."[304]

"Know that enjoining righteousness and forbidding evil does not reduce the provision or shorten the term of life."[305]

"The compassionate is he who comes to the one who shunned him. The granter of favor is he who extends the favor before he is asked for it."[306]

"Do not seek to know the truth according to other people. Rather first come to know the Truth, for only then will you recognize its people."[307]

He also said, "By Allah, unity is with the consensus/Ijma' of the people of truth even though they may be few while disunity is the consensus of the people of falsehood even though they may be many."[308]

"When a word comes from the heart, it falls onto the heart; but when it comes from the tongue, it will go no farther than the ears."[309]

"There is nothing good in this world except one of two people: 1) a person who commits a sin and then hastens to erase it by repenting, and 2) a person who strives to do good."[310]

"O! world! Get away from me. Do you want to fool me? Or are you eager for me? You can never do that. Go and fool someone else. I do not need you. I have divorced you, and will never return to you. Life in you is short, and your problems are too many. Your ambitions are base. O' how little are the provisions for and how far the trip is; how great is the entrance place, and how rough is the place to sleep!"[311]

To continue, Allah ﷻ says, "*Is he then who guides to the truth more worthy to be followed or he who himself does not go aright unless he is guided? What then is the matter with you, how do you judge?*"[312]

These verses were very relevant to Sayyiduna ʿAli ﷺ and they touched him to the point that he would be extremely cautious and he would often be heard reciting, *"My Lord, I seek refuge with You from asking You of that which I have no knowledge. If You do not forgive me and have mercy on me, I shall be among the losers."*[313]

Sayyiduna Ali ibn Abi Talib ﷺ was once asked a question, he replied by saying, "I have no knowledge on the subject." He then said, "what a great source of comfort! I was questioned about something I did not know and I acknowledged that I did not know."[314]

He would also recite, "Glory be to You, we have no knowledge except what you have taught us. Truly, it is You who are, the All-Knowing, the All-Wise."[315]

Allah ﷺ says, *"To Allah is your ultimate return, then He will inform you of every thing you disputed."*[316]

"Say: 'Tell me, what do you think about the things Allah has sent down to you as provision, which you have now attested to saying, they are lawful and unlawful?'"[317]

"Do not say about what your lying tongues describe: "This is permissible and this is not permissible, inventing lies against Allah."[318] and other similar verses.

Sayyiduna ʿAli ibn Abi Talib's ﷺ protection of knowledge and fear of giving false information was because of his love for Allah ﷺ and his Messenger ﷺ and he took on the traits of the Messenger of Allah and taught exactly in the same manner.

He said, "Whenever I used to hear a narration from the Prophet ﷺ, Allah would cause me to benefit by it however He willed. If anyone informed me of any statement that he said, I would make him swear that the Prophet ﷺ said it. If he swore by Allah, then I would believe him. [Sayyiduna] Abu Bakr [as-Siddique] ﷺ, once told me, and please remember Abu Bakr was truthful — that he heard the Messenger of Allah ﷺ say, "There is not any Muslim who commits a sin, then he makes Wudhu and prays two units of prayer, except that he will be forgiven."[319]

He was very serious about knowledge and the Prophet himself ﷺ was the medium of Sayyiduna ʿAli ؑ and there is nothing strange about this relationship. That is the way of traditional Islam, we learn through heart to heart transmission, which far outweighs any book knowledge attained by other means.

These scholars of the heart are, "*Those who actively listen to the teachings of Allah and obey his commands prosper and are saved.*"[320]

"Those who listen to the Word, and follow the best of it: those are the ones who Allah has guided, and those are the ones endowed with understanding."[321]

Shaykh Muhammad ibn al-Munkadir ؒ,[322] said: "A scholar is the medium between Allah and His servants, so the scholar should be careful about how to convey the message."[323]

In relation to how Sayyiduna ʿAli ؑ treated people, he followed the Sunnah of the Prophet ﷺ and he would mirror him, in that he never used his knowledge for his own selfish purposes either. He was also very easy on people in regard to his legal rulings. He once said, "Indeed, the scholar is he who does not let the people fall into despair about the the Mercy of Allah and he who does not make them feel secure against the Plan of Allah."[324]

Much more can be said, yet brevity is the Sunnah and with Allah ﷻ is the Success.

Extra Benefit Two

Allah says, *"Say! 'Are those who know and those who do not know alike?'"*[325] and, *"Is He then Who guides to the truth more worthy to be followed, or he who himself does not go aright unless he is guided? What then is the matter with you; how do you judge?"*[326]

Reflecting upon the above, it now has to be noted, that Sayyiduna ʿAli ibn Abi Talib ﷺ was the chief Jurist [*Faqi*] and chief judge [*Qadi*] among the Companions [*Sahaba*].

His knowledge of Fiqh was so vast that he said: "Shall I not tell you who the real professor of law [*Faqih*] is? He is one who does not make people despair of the mercy of Allah, yet he does not give them concessions to disobey Allah either. He does not make them feel safe from the plan of Allah and he does not leave the Quran. There is no good in worship that involves no efforts to gain knowledge of law [*Fiqh*], and there is no good in seeking Fiqh without seeking a thorough understanding. And there is no good in reading without contemplating."[327]

He also would say, "Narrate to people what they can understand; do you want Allah and His Messenger to be disbelieved in?"[328]

Hafiz ibn Hajr al-Asqalani 🕮, explains, "In this narration there is evidence that ambiguous knowledge should not be mentioned among the common people/general public."[329]

ʿAbdullah ibn Masud 🕮 narrated that the Prophet Muhammad 🕮 said: "They are the losers, those who make the religion hard and tough. They imperil themselves who enforce tough practices of Islam. They destroy themselves, those who go to extremes."[330]

This is in accordance with other similar Hadith where the Messenger of Allah 🕮 says, "Make things easy for the people, and do not make it difficult for them, and make them calm and do not repulse them."[331] and "Make people happy and do not scare them; make things easy for them and do not make things difficult."[332]

Anas ibn Malik 🕮 narrated that the Messenger of Allah 🕮 said, "The most merciful one in my nation towards my community is Abu Bakr, the most severe between them in religious matters is ʿUmar, the most truthful one is ʿUthman, the best judge from among them is ʿAli, the best reciter of the Book of Allah among them is Ubayy ibn Kaʾb, the most knowledgeable in regard to the Halal and Haram is Muadh ibn Jabal, most knowledgeable in matters of inheritance is Zayd ibn Thabit. Attention! Each nation had his own Ameen (trusty), and the trusty of this nation is Abu Ubaydah ibn al-Jarrah."[333]

All of the Sahaba learned the importance of seeking knowledge with Sayyiduna ʿAli ibn Abi Talib 🕮 by the Prophet 🕮 himself. Caliph ʿUmar ibn al-Khattab 🕮 for example, said: "ʿAli, is best judge between us."[334]

Imam Jalaluddin as-Suyuti 🕮, relates in his History of the Caliphs:[335] "Caliph ʿUmar ibn al-Khattab 🕮 during his time as rule as the Caliph would famously say, "If it were not for ʿAli, ʿUmar would have been ruined."[336] and "I seek the help of Allah in deciding those difficult problems for which Abul-Hasan is not available to answer."[337]

ʿAbdullah ibn Abbas 🕮 said: "If a ruling would reach us narrated by the trustworthy from ʿAli, we wouldn't leave that Fatwa for other ruling."[338]

In another saying with a Sahih chain, it is related that "When 'Ali died, his son Imam al-Hasan, Allah ennoble their countenance, delivered a sermon to us on the death of Ali, saying: 'Yesterday, you were separated from a man who none from the past ever surpassed in knowledge and whom none will ever equal in knowledge.'"[339]

Imam Yahya ibn Sa'id ♦, relates: "There was not a single man from the companions who could say: 'Ask me', except 'Ali ibn Abi Talib."[340]

Sayyiduna 'Ali ♦ said himself: "The Prophet of Allah ♦ enlightened me on one thousand branches of knowledge, each branch opening a thousand gates (in itself) on learning."[341]

On another occasion he is known to have said: "Whatever I hear, I never forgot and never will forget."[342] and this is why the Sahaba agree, "No one but 'Ali ibn Abi Talib was able to assert on the pulpit, publicly that he could answer any question and explain any subject with respect to the contents of the Holy Quran," and there is another saying, which reads, "O people! Ask me since after me you will never find anyone more knowledgeable than me to pose questions. Neither will you find anyone more knowledgeable than me about what is between the two covers (the Holy Quran). So ask me."[343]

Allah ♦ says, "*He gives wisdom unto whom He wills, and he unto whom wisdom is given, he truly has received abundant good. But none remember except men of understanding.*"[344]

To name some of the other Judges among the Sahaba of that time who sought the knowledge of Sayyiduna 'Ali ibn Abi Talib ♦, there is the narration of the Hadith Master 'Ali ibn al-Madani (one of the teachers of Imam Bukhari), Allah have Mercy upon them, who said, "It is common for it to be said: The Muslim Ummah has four judges and they are, 'Umar ibn al-Khattab, 'Ali ibn Abi Talib, Zayd ibn Thabit, and Abu Musa al-Ash'ari ♦."[345]

He[346] also says that Masruq ♦, said: "I studied the companions of the Prophet Muhammad ♦ and found that six of them had gathered together all their knowledge: 'Umar, 'Ali, 'Abdullahi ibn Mas'ud, Abu ad-Darda', Ubayy ibn Ka'b and Zayd ibn Thabit ♦." Then I studied these six and found that their knowledge was from two of them: 'Ali and 'Abdullahi ibn Mas'ud ♦."[347]

To end, the knowledge and wisdom of Sayyiduna ʿAli ibn Abi Talib ﷺ was beyond comparison. For example, Kumayl ibn Ziyad an-Nakha'i ﷺ, reported:

ʿAli ﷺ took me by the hand and brought me to the outskirts of the desert. When we reached there he sat down. After catching his breath he said, "O Kumayl, hearts are vessels [for knowledge], and the best of them are those that contain the most.

Memorize what I say to you. People can be divided into one of three classes:

1. Punctilious people of knowledge [who practice what they know]

2. People of knowledge who continuously remain learning as their means of salvation,

3. Hooligans who follow any and everybody along with the passing wind; they are not enlightened by knowledge and they do not have any reliable source to refer to [in religious matters]. Knowledge is better than wealth because while knowledge guards you, you must guard your wealth. Furthermore, knowledge accumulates with practice, while wealth depletes with usage. Loving the scholar is part of practicing Deen."[348]

Here ends this section on the Knowledge and Wisdom of ʿAli ibn Abi Talib. Much more could have been said, yet brevity is the Sunnah and with Allah ﷻ is the Success.

Extra Benefit Three

SAYYIDUNA ʿALI — ONE OF THE TOP
SPIRITUAL MASTERS OF THE MUSLIMS

All of the teachings from the Prophet Muhammad ﷺ made ʿAli one of the Top Spiritual Masters of the Muslims.

After reflecting upon all these sayings of the Prophet Muhammad ﷺ, it is clear that Sayyiduna ʿAli ؓ said, had gained the rank of having a close friendship of Allah [Wilayah of Allah].

Sayyiduna ʿAli ibn Abi Talib ؓ said, "My affection doesn't move toward anything except by His wind, and the captain of my cavalry is nothing except love for the One."[349]

This Wilayah in general is important to the one on the path of righteousness. It is as Shaykh Mukhtar al-Kunti ؓ, said: "Wilayah' (the state of friendship with Allah) is attained in three ways: 1) it is inherited [*wiraatha*]; 2) it may come through unexpected divine attraction [*jadhb*]; and 3) through spiritual discipline and struggle [*riyaada wa mujaahida*].

As for the first, he/she is the one who inherited Wilayah from a saintly mother, father, or grandparent. This is corroborated by the words of Allah TaʾAla: "*Indeed I am making you an Imam. He said: 'And for my descendants?' He said: 'My covenant will not reach the unjust among them.'"* Thus, a prophet, scholar, or Muslim sage can supplicate Allah taʿala to make his descendants inherit their spiritual stations, since as he upon him be peace once said: "The supplication of the parent for its child is answered." As for the second manner of attaining Wilayah it is through an unintentional inadvertent spiritual attraction [*jadhb*], like what happened with al-Khidr, upon him be peace and many others.

In fact all '*Awliyah*' go through some form of '*jadhb*', even if it is a moment. '*Jadhb*' is a magnetic spiritual attraction which comes from Allah, and not the servant, and is often described as a form of spiritual intoxication similar to what happened to the Messenger at the moment revelation descended. The third manner is through the well known spiritual discipline and struggle, where the servant disciplines himself/ herself with the bridle of taqwa, and she/he continues to perform extra acts of worship until Allah loves him, and when He loves, a transformation occurs which was corroborated by the well known Hadith Qudsi where Allah says: "*I become the sight by which he sees.*". And Allah knows best.[350]

Now let us look at the meaning of another word Mawla, because it comes from the root word Wilayah.

In the Hans Wehr Arabic Dictionary: "The word "Mawla" itself is composed from the morpheme indicating place, lit. 'noun of place' (*ism al-makan*) and derives from the root word waliya (masdar/verbal noun: al-wilayah) classically translated as "to be proximal" [to both parties in a vertical relationship] or "to intercede". Thus the semantic translation of mawla most closely resembles the phrase "place of intercession. It has the meaning of master, lord, protector, patron, client, charge, friend, companion, and associate."[351]

Within the Science of Tasawwuf/Sufism the definition of a Mawla is a spiritual protector or saint. "It is spelled mawlay, moulay, or mulay within the region of Northern Africa [al-Maghrib] and Andalusia. In Morocco, it refers to descendants of the Prophet Muhammad ﷺ."[352]

In regard to Sayyiduna ʿAli ؑ being a spiritual master [*mawla*] among the Muslims, the following Hadith are examples as well, "The one who wants to live my life and die my death will attach himself to

ʿAli."[353] and "Whomsoever took me as a master, then ʿAli is also his master (*Mawla*)."[354]

And with that said, let us now look at the Event of Ghadeer Khum. Much more can be said, yet brevity is Sunnah and with Allah ﷻ is the Success.

Extra Benefit Four

SAYYIDUNA ʿALI IBN ABI TALIB AND
THE SPIRITUAL SIGNIFICANCE OF
THE EVENT OF GHADEER KHUM

Allah ﷻ says, "*Truly! Indeed, the friends of Allah there is no concern for them, and they do not grieve. The friends of Allah are those who believe and are fearfully aware.*"[355]

Imam an-Nasa'i ﷺ, records in his Sunan al-Kubra, "When the Messenger of Allah returned from the last Hajj, he then came down [rested] at Ghadeer Khumm and "Then he declared: 'I am about to answer the call (of death). Truly, I have left two precious things [*Thaqalayn*] among you, one of which is greater than the other: the Book of Allah and my ʿItrah, my Ahlul Bayt. So watch out how you treat them after me. For, indeed, they will never separate until they return to me by the side of the Pond.' Then he said, 'Verily, Allah is my master [*Mawlaya*] and I am the Wali of every believer.' Then he took ʿAli's hand and declared, 'To whomever I am his master, this one is also his master. May Allah, befriend whoever befriends him and be hostile to whoever is hostile to him.'" Abu Tufayl says: "I said to Zayd, 'Did you hear it from the Prophet ﷺ?' He replied, 'There was no one in the caravan who did not see it with his eyes and hear it with his ears".[356]

ʿAli is also a master [*Mawla*] in a spiritual sense, meaning if we follow him as a master, He will lead us to Allah, and this is why the Prophet, at the beginning of Ghadeer Khutbah during the Farewell Hajj addressed the people: Do I not have more authority on you more than what you have on yourself? They said: Of course? Then he said: Of whomsoever I am the master; then ʿAli is also his master."[357]

This is the Event where Caliph ʿUmar ibn al-Khattab met up with Sayyiduna ʿAli and said to him: "O son of Abu Talib! Congratulations, you have become the master of every male and female believer, morning and evening (for ever)."[358] [359]

This is also the day Allah commanded, "*O Prophet! Deliver what has been sent down to you from your Lord; and if you don't do it, you have not delivered His message; and Allah will protect you from the people.*"[360]

Allah also Revealed on this day, "I have perfected for you your religion and I have given you of My highest favors. I have chosen Islam as your way of life."[361]

Imam al-Bukhari, also relates, that at the end of his the farewell sermon [*Khutbah*], the Prophet said twice:

"Behold! Haven't I conveyed the message of Allah?" or "It is incumbent upon every one who is present to inform the absent for they may understand it better than those who are present".[362]

Now with that said, the above needs to be put into perspective. It is important to note a narration by Imam al-Bayhaqi, who said that a man said, "I heard al-Hasan ibn al-Hasan, the brother of ʿAbd Allah ibn al-Hasan while he was saying to a man who was among their lovers" He said: "One day a Rafidi (one who rejects the Caliphate of the first 3 Caliphs) said to him, "Didn't the Messenger of Allah say, 'Whosoever I am his Mawla, Ali too is his Mawla'?" So, he [al-Hasan] replied, "I swear by Allah, if the Messenger of Allah, had intended with that authority and government over the people after him, he would have stated it more clearly, as he stated to them clearly about Salat, Zakat, the fast of the month of Ramadan, and the Hajj to the House. He would have said to them, "Truly, this one is your Wali al-'Amr [chief ruler] after me. Therefore, listen to him and obey him."[363]

Now that the above is cleared up, we know have to ask ourselves; why would the Prophet Muhammad 💧 make such great statements concerning Sayyiduna ʿAli being a spiritual master if they were not true?

The Prophet 💧 would not lie of course, for he is al-Amin, the most-trustworthy among the creation of Allah 💧. Thus, the conclusion must be that the Messenger of Allah 💧 knew that ʿAli was meant for greatness and in greatness comes many trials. Some of these trials were very similar those endured by Jesus the son of Mary [Eesa ibn Maryam], Peace be upon them.

Allah 💧 says concerning this, "*And when the son of Maryam is cited as an example, behold, people make mockery of it.*"[364]

The Prophet 💧 is also known to have said, as is narrated on the authority of Abu Hurayrah 💧[365] "Out of everyone, I am the closest to Jesus, the son of Mary, among all of mankind, concerning this worldly life and the hereafter. The Companions said: O! Messenger of Allah in what way do you mean? Thereupon the Messenger of Allah said: The Prophets are brothers in faith, having different mothers. However, their religion is one and there is no Prophet between myself and Jesus."[366]

Now, as we look at the above, it is very significant to note that Sayyiduna ʿAli tells us, "The Messenger of Allah 💧 called me and told me: "You are similar to Jesus,[367] the Jews hated him to the point that they slandered his mother, and the Christians loved him to the point that they put him in a position that is not suited for him."[368]

Sayyiduna ʿAli 💧 himself said: "With regard to me, two categories of people will be ruined, namely he who loves me too much and the love takes him away from rightfulness, and he who hates me too much and the hatred takes him away from rightfulness. Verily, I am not a Prophet, and there is nothing revealed to me. But I work with the Book of Allah and the Sunnah of his Prophet as much as I can. So whatever I have asked you in regard of obeying Allah, it is your duty to obey me whether you like it or not."[369]

This is a clear sign for those who reflect upon the above, that there is no problem in taking ʿAli as one's Mawla. We follow Sayyiduna ʿAli because in this way we are connecting our spiritual chain [*Silsilah*] back to the Prophet ﷺ. Every spiritual path within Tasawwuf does this and this is nothing that needs to be defended, for it is well known. The problem that occurs is when people place Sayyiduna ʿAli into a godly realm, calling him a Prophet or Allah himself. These of course being unfounded, mythical beliefs. We can only accept what is founded in traditional, logical Deen and we ask Allah ﷻ that He give us true love of ʿAli in this regard. Amin.

In connecting ourselves to Sayyiduna ʿAli ؑ we are actually obeying and heeding the Commandment of Allah ﷻ to align ourselves with the blessed person of the Messenger of Allah ﷺ, for he is our leader and we need his intercession on the Day of Judgment.

We must remember that Allah ﷻ says, "We will call forth for judgment [on the Day of Reckoning] every community of people in accordance to the leadership that they designated for themselves."[370]

"For, one Day, We shall raise from every community a leading witness against them from among themselves. And We shall call you to testify regarding those whom your Message has reached. The Book We have revealed to you explains everything; a Guide and Grace and the glad tiding for Muslims."[371]

Truly, the Prophet Muhammad ﷺ is the master of us all of course, yet he passed on his walking example of the Quran, to ʿAli who is the manifestation of spiritual excellence in the flesh. May Allah send peace and blessings upon the entire family of the Prophet and grant them the highest ranks of Jannah. Amin.

Extra Benefit Five

THE GOOD RELATIONS BETWEEN SAYYIDUNA ʿALI AND THE FIRST THREE CALIPHS

Anas ibn Malik ؓ narrates that the Prophet ﷺ was once sitting in the Masjid with the Companions [*Sahaba*] around him. ʿAli then arrived, greeted everyone with the greetings of peace [*Salam*] and then stood there to look for a place to sit. The Prophet ﷺ looked at the faces of the Sahaba to see which of them would make a place for him. Sayyiduna Abu Bakr as-Siddique ؓ, who was sitting on the Prophet's ﷺ right side, then shifted from his place and said, "Come here [and sit], O Abul Hasan." ʿAli then sat between the beloved Prophet ﷺ and Abu Bakr as-Siddique. The Sahaba could see the happiness on the face of the Prophet ﷺ as he said to Abu Bakr as-Siddique, "O Abu Bakr! It is only the people of virtue who recognize others of virtue."[372]

We have to know that the Messenger of Allah ﷺ loves the Muhajirun and the Ansar among the Sahaba and he also leaned towards them, as is proven in a narration of Abu Saʾid al-Khudri ؓ

The Messenger of Allah ﷺ said: "Indeed my elite, those whom I lean towards, are the people of my inner house [*Ahlul-Bayt*] and my close ones are the helpers of Madinah [*Ansar*], so forgive those who do wrong from them and accept from those who do good from them."[373]

Allah ﷻ speaks of this within the Quran, "Surely those who believed and immigrated and struggled hard in the path of Allah with their property and their souls, and those who gave shelter and helped—these are guardians, friends [*Awliyah*] of each other."[374]

With the reflection of the above, we ask Allah to give us all a deep belief, love and respect for Allah ﷻ, the Messenger of Allah ﷺ, his family [*Ahlul Baytihi*] and the companions [*Sahaba*], for they are as the lights that guide the travelers within the deepest mines and caves.

Sayyidi Shaykh Muhammad ibn Ibrahim al-Yaqoubi, May Allah preserve him, once said, "Unfortunately in today's society, especially in the way Islam has been spread in the west, makes it almost strange that we talk about the family of the Prophet ﷺ. I don't know why? Well, I may say it is because of ignorance, but it shouldn't be this way. Throughout our history, the Ahlul-Bayt were always revered and respected by the Ahlus Sunnah."

Sayyidi Shaykh Muhammad ibn Yayha an-Ninowi, May Allah preserve him, commented, "But because it's a sensitive issue, then you don't want to go there, however we need them. We need Ahlul-Bayt in our lives. Because they are the second weight that the Prophet ﷺ left us and told us specifically that if you hold on to them you will not be misguided."

Many of the top ranking Sahaba knew very well the high status of the family of the Messenger of Allah ﷺ. They were not unaware of the sayings of the Prophet ﷺ in regard to them. It would be foolish to think so.

For example, Sayyiduna Abu Bakr loved Sayyiduna ʿAli ؓ so much that he was continuously looking at his face, and so his daughter ʿAisha ؓ asked "Oh my father why is that you like to stare at the face of ʿAli?

Caliph Abu Bakr as-Siddique ؓ replied, "Oh my daughter, do you not know? [I swear] By Allah who has my soul in his hand, I heard the Prophet ﷺ say that to look at the face of ʿAli is worship."[375]

Caliph Abu Bakr as-Siddique also said, "It would be difficult indeed for anyone to pass through the Bridge of Sirat, on the Day of

Judgment without getting a permit to pass from ʿAli, because this is what the Messenger of Allah ﷺ told me about this?"[376]

The full story is also narrated, "One day Sayyiduna Abu Bakr ؓ saw ʿAli and smiled. ʿAli looked at Abu Bakr and asked him the reason for the smile. Abu Bakr said, "O, ʿAli!, Congratulations. I have heard the Prophet ﷺ say that nobody will be able to cross the Bridge of Sirat without getting the permission of ʿAli."

[After hearing this], Sayyiduna ʿAli smiled at this and said, "O Leader of the Believers [Amir al-Mu'minin] ؓ, congratulations to you as well. Because the Prophet ﷺ has told me the same about you. He said, ʿAli, you will only give permission to those who truly love Abu Bakr and do not give permission to anyone who has even the slightest bit of hatred towards Abu Bakr."[377]

A good example of Sayyiduna ʿAli ibn Abi Talib ؓ using his wisdom is when he helped Caliph ʿUmar ؓ as is related by the Great Jurist of Madinah, Imam Saʿid ibn al-Musayyib, who said: "The first one to establish the Hijri calendar was ʿUmar ibn al-Khattab[378] two and a half years into his Caliphate. He reached a decision in consultation with ʿAli ibn Abi Talib ؓ."[379]

ʿAbdullah ibn Abbas ؓ said, "If all the trees and gardens turn into pens and the oceans into ink and the jinn into accountants and men into scribes, they will be unable to enumerate the merits of [Sayyiduna] ʿAli ibn Abi Talib ؓ."[380]

Caliph ʿUmar ibn al-Khattab ؓ and his family felt the same about ʿAli as is shown in a narration from Saʿd ibn ʿUbaydah ؓ who narrated that a man came to ʿAbdullah ibn ʿUmar ؓ and asked about ʿUthman ibn Affan and Ibn ʿUmar ؓ mentioned his good deeds and said to the questioner. "Perhaps these facts annoy you?" The other said, "Yes." Ibn ʿUmar said, "May Allah stick your nose in the dust!'

Then the man asked him about ʿAli. Ibn ʿUmar ؓ mentioned his good deeds and said, "It is all true, and that is his house in the midst of the houses of the Prophet. Perhaps these facts have hurt you?" The questioner said, "Yes." Ibn ʿUmar said, "May Allah stick your nose in the dust! Go away and do whatever you can against me." May Allah be pleased with them.[381]

On another occasion Caliph ʿUmar bin Khattab narrates that the Prophet ﷺ said, "Indeed, Fatimah, Ali, Hasan and Husayn will live in a white dome in Paradise. The Throne of Rahman will be its roof ﷺ."[382]

"It is narrated by ʿUmar ibn al-Khattab ﷺ, that once two Bedouins came to him disputing with each other. He said to ʿAli: O Abul-Hasan: decide between these two. So he decided between them (and settled their dispute). One of them said: Is he (ʿAli) the only one left to decide between us? and pointed towards ʿAli and said: this pot-bellied person (will decide between us)! ʿUmar rose from his seat, caught him by the collar, lifted him from the ground and said: May you be dead! Do you know that the person you consider worthless is my master [*Mawla*] and the master of every believer."[383]

On the other end of the spectrum of this extremism, there are those who claim to be supporters and lovers of Sayyiduna ʿAli, however they do not even respect those whom Allah and his Messenger love.

They deny the fact that the Messenger of Allah ﷺ said, "Stick to the two after me, Abu Bakr and ʿUmar."[384] And then claim any whom reject the hatred of them as those who do not know History. This is trickery and do not be fooled by such dealings. The Messenger of Allah loved them and they loved him back.

A perfect example of being balanced is within a narration of Muhammad ibn al-Hanafiyyah (the son of ʿAli), Allah be pleased with him. He said: I said to my father: Which of the people after the Messenger of Allah ﷺ is best? He replied: Abu Bakr. I then asked: Who comes next? He said: ʿUmar. I was then afraid of asking him who came next, and he might mention ʿUthman, so I said: You came next, O my father? He said: I am only a man among the Muslims.[385]

Sayyiduna ʿAli ibn Abi Talib ﷺ, himself narrated that the Prophet ﷺ said: "May Allah have mercy on Abu Bakr. He married me to his daughter, took me the the Abode of Hijrah, and freed Bilal ﷺ with his own property. May Allah have mercy on ʿUmar. He speaks the truth, even if it's bitter and the truth has left him without a friend. May Allah have mercy on Uthman. The angels are shy before him. May Allah have mercy on Ali. O Allah, make the truth go wherever he goes."[386]

Imam Bukhari ﷺ, narrated from ibn Abbas, Allah be pleased with him: "ʿUmar was lying on the place (for washing). People rounded him from four sides. They started invoking and praying for him, when he wasn't raised yet. And I was between them. Man behind me rested his elbows on my shoulders, that was Ali. He asked mercy for him, and said: "You didn't left behind you someone, than yourself, with whose deeds I more wish to face with Allah. By Allah, I always hoped that Allah will keep you with your two companions, for I often heard the Messenger of Allah ﷺ saying, "I, Abu Bakr and ʿUmar were (somewhere). I, Abu Bakr and ʿUmar did (something). I, Abu Bakr and ʿUmar set out."[387]

For example the Messenger of Allah ﷺ said, "Truly, Allah has placed the truth upon the tongue & heart of Umar."[388]

Another example of Sayyiduna ʿAli's praise, is narrated by Abu Sariha who said: I heard ʿAli ibn Abi Talib ﷺ saying on the pulpit: "Indeed Abu Bakr was a very kind hearted person and truly ʿUmar was one who always wanted things to go well in regard to the Deen of Allah. For this reason Allah always blessed him with good." (Allah be pleased with them all).[389]

Many others are related in praise of Abu Bakr and ʿUthman as well, thus how does one deem it permissible to slander the Sahaba? Abu Bakr was the best friend of the Messenger of Allah ﷺ and the first to lead Salat after his death. ʿAisha was the wife of the Messenger of Allah and is considered of one the top scholars of all time, ʿUthman Dhun Nurayn ibn Affan ﷺ married two daughters of the Messenger of Allah ﷺ and the list goes on and on. Now in regard to the Companions one has to remember that in general,

Allah ﷻ says, "Muhammad is the Messenger of Allah ﷺ, and those who are with him (the Companions) are severe against disbelievers, and merciful among themselves. You see them bowing and falling down prostrate (in prayer), seeking Bounty from Allah and (His) Good Pleasure. The mark of them (i.e. of their faith) is no their faces (foreheads) from the traces of (their) prostration (during prayers)."[390]

In another Hadith the Messenger of Allah ﷺ said: "The best of my Ummah (nation) are the people of my era (the Companions), then those who are after them (the Followers), then those who are after them (Followers of the Followers). Thereafter, will be such people who will bear testimony where their testimony will not be needed; they will be deceptive and untrustworthy; and they will make vows but will never fulfill them."[391]

In an another authentic saying on the authority of Hilal bin Khabab from al-Hassan ibn Muhammad bin al-Hanafiyyah ﷺ that he said: "O you, who reside in Kufa, Iraq; fear Allah and do not say bad things about Abu Bakr and ʿUmar, for truly it is Abu Bakr as-Siddique ﷺ who was the second of the two in the cave with the Prophet ﷺ and as for ʿUmar ﷺ Allah had strengthened our Islam with ʿUmar."[392]

There is an authentic narration from Salim bin Abi Hafsah who asks the Imam Jafar as-Sadiq, about Abu Bakr as-Siddique and ʿUmar ibn al-Khattab, Allah is pleased with them: Jafar bin Muhammad told me: "O Salim, Abu Bakr as-Siddique is my grandfather, what man in his right mind would insult his own grandfather?" (Allah be pleased with them).

He also told me in an authentic chain of narration: "May the intercession of the Prophet Muhammad ﷺ never reach me on the day of judgement, if I am not loyal to them (Sayyiduna Abu Bakr and ʿUmar) and if I do not disassociate myself from their enemies".

There is also from Imam al-Hakim an-Nishapuri in his al-Mustadarak an authentic narration from Imam Jafar bin Muhammad as-Sadiq, from his father Imam Muhammad bin Ali al-Baqir, from Abdullah ibn Jafar ibn Abi Talib ﷺ that he said: "Sayyiduna Abu Bakr as-Siddique, Allah is pleased with him, became our Caliph and he was from among the best of the Caliphs of Allah, he was most merciful and most caring towards us."

Another Hadith on the Virtues of the first three Caliphs is, Anas ibn Malik narrated that the Prophet ﷺ climbed Uhud with Abu Bakr, ʿUmar and ʿUthman, and it trembled beneath them. He said, ʿStand firm, O Uhud, for there is no one on you but a Prophet, a Siddeeq and two martyrs."[393]

"The most correct of what I have come across is that a Sahabi (Companion) is one who met the Prophet whilst believing in him, and died as a Muslim. So that includes the one who remained with him for a long or a short time, and those who narrated from him and those who did not, and those who saw him but did not sit with him and those who could not see him due to blindness."[394]

Therefore anyone who curses the Companions or speaks ill of them are from among the following: "Surely, those who annoy Allah and His Messenger are cursed by Allah in this world and the Hereafter, and He has prepared for them a humiliating punishment."[395]

To be clear, The Aqeedah (belief system) of the true follower of the Sunnah, is that we obey the Quran and the Hadith from the Messenger of Allah ﷺ such as, "Allah, Allah! Fear Him with regard to my Companions/Sahaba! Do not make them targets after me! Whoever loves them loves them with his love for me; and whoever hates them hates them with his hatred for me. Whoever bears enmity for them, bears enmity for me; and whoever bears enmity for me, bears enmity for Allah. Whoever bears enmity for Allah is about to perish!"[396]

This is because Allah ﷻ says, "You [the Companions] are the best of peoples ever raised for mankind, you enjoin good and forbid evil, and you believe in Allah."[397]

Allah ﷻ also says, "And the first to embrace Islam of those who migrated from Mecca to Madinah [*Muhajirun*] and the helpers of Madinah [*Ansar*] and also those who followed them exactly. Allah is well-pleased with them as they are well pleased with Him. He has prepared for them Gardens under which rivers flow, to dwell therein forever. That is the supreme success."[398]

The great jurist of the Shafi School, Imam an-Nawawi ؒ, explains: "Know that to insult the Companions is prohibited and constitutes one of the grave prohibited indecencies [*al-Fawahish al-Muharramat*] whether with regard to those of them involved in a dissension or other than them, because they entered those conflicts on the conviction of their independent judgment [*Ijtihad*] and interpretation."[399]

Umm al-Mu'minin ʿAisha ؓ was once told, "Some people are criticizing the Companions of the Messenger of Allah, even Abu Bakr and ʿUmar." She responded by saying, "Do not be surprised by this! Their ability to work good deeds has been cut off (because of returning to Allah), however Allah has preferred that their reward shall not be cut off."[400]

Therefore, you have to ask yourselves, why would anyone do this when it is known that Sayyiduna ʿAli himself has a son named Abu Bakr he said concerning Abu Bakr and ʿUmar 🙵?

"Whoever says that I have a greater rank than Abu Bakr and ʿUmar, I shall punish him with the punishment [*Hadd*] of a slanderer."[401]

Sayyiduna ʿAli 🙵 also said: "Am I anything other than a part of the goodness of Abu Bakr as-Siddique?"[402] You have to remember that Sayyiduna Abu Bakr as-Siddique was the best friend of the Messenger of Allah 🙵 his whole life and ʿAli was in close contact with him from childhood. Thus, the lie of them hating one another is a gross one indeed.

It is related by the historians al-Yaqubi and al-Masudi, "The first, main proof that Sayyiduna ʿAli ibn Abi Talib 🙵 loved Abu Bakr as-Siddique is because he named one of his own sons Abu Bakr. His sons followed right in his footsteps; because both Imams al-Hasan and al-Husayn had sons named Abu Bakr."[403] (Allah be pleased with them).

Another good example is within the following where Suwayd ibn Ghaflah said: 'I entered on ʿAli ibn Abi Talib 🙵 during his emirate and said: "I passed by some folks who were talking about Abu Bakr and ʿUmar and saying that you have a deep hatred for both of them, one of those folks is ʿAbdullah ibn Saba, ʿAli said: "I do not understand this wicked man (Ibn Saba), I seek refuge in Allah from this matter and I only have deep beautiful respect for them. Then he sent after Ibn Saba and exiled him to al-Madaen, Yemen and said: "He will not live in the same land with me." He then went to his Mimbar and when the people gathered he complimented both of them and said nothing but good things about them. then he said: "If it reaches me that anyone prefers me over them (Shaykhayn) then I shall lash them as they do with the slandering liar."[404]

To quote some of the greatest Imams on the matter:

Imam Ahmad ibn Hanbal 🙵, would say, "The Companions of the Messenger of Allah 🙵 after the four caliphs—are the best of the people, and it is not permissible for anyone to speak ill of any of them, blaming them for deficiencies and shortcomings."[405]

Imam al-Azam Abu Hanifah ﷺ, said, "We love the Companions of the Messenger of Allah ﷺ but we do not go to excess in our love for any one individual among them nor do we disown any one of them. We hate anyone who hates them or does not speak well of them."[406]

Imam Malik ibn Anas ﷺ, had an even sterner stance because he deemed anyone who reviled a companion to be going against the following verse, "that He (Allah) may enrage the disbelievers with them."[407]

Sayyiduna ʿAli ﷺ had the above love for the Companions and they in turn loved he and his family back. Even if they disagreed on certain matters it did not mean they were at the necks of each other, or threatening in the least bit. This happened with the start of the Ummayid monarchy and we won't go there. This book is to stay within the mines of the Virtues of Sayyiduna ʿAli, Allah ennoble his countenance.

An example of this can be seen when Sayyiduna ʿAli ibn Abi Talib ﷺ came to ʿUmar ibn al-Khattab while he was sitting in his place of gathering [*Majlis*], so when ʿUmar saw him he became extremely humble, then he moved to offer him a comfortable place to sit. Later on when ʿAli left the gathering, some of the people asked ʿUmar: "O Leader of the Believers, you treat ʿAli unlike anyone from among the companions of our beloved Prophet Muhammad?"

ʿUmar said to the man: "How do you think my behavior towards him was like?"

The man said: "I noticed that whenever you would look at him, you then become muddled and you humbled yourself, choosing himself over you because you are the one that moved to the side so that he may sit comfortably."

ʿUmar ﷺ said: "And so what? What's preventing me from doing so? By Allah, he is my leader/Mawla and the chief/Mawla of every believer."[408]

Imam Jafar as-Sadiq 🕮 relates from his father, that when ʿUmar ibn al-Khattab 🕮, wanted to distribute the Khums among the people, and he was the best of them in opinion, they said:"Begin with yourself." So he said: "No, I begin with those closest to the Prophet." So he distributed the Khums to Prophet's uncle al-ʿAbbas, then to ʿAli, and continued to do so for every tribe until he ended with Bani ʿAdi bin Kab."[409]

The moral of the story is that the family of the Messenger of Allah 🕮 and the first 3 Caliphs may have had differences of opinion over certain matters, yet they never rebelled and they actually had a very good relationship with one another and they all treated one another as if they were all each others masters. None saw themselves more praiseworthy than the other. And Allah Knows Best. Some claim the difference ʿAli had with ʿUthman prove that he thought he should have been the ruler other than Caliph ʿUthman. These types of thoughts are unfounded and spread by the Khawariji influence, for as was noted ʿAli was a vizier of ʿUthman as well and did not rebel against him.

ʿAbdullah ibn ʿAbbas 🕮 narrated: While I was standing among the people who were invoking Allah for Umar bin Al-Khattab 🕮 who was lying (dead) on his bed, a man behind me rested his elbows on my shoulder and said, "(O ʿUmar!) May Allah bestow His Mercy on you. I always hoped that Allah will keep you with your two companions, for I often heard the Messenger of Allah saying, "I, Abu Bakr and ʿUmar were (somewhere). I, Abu Bakr and ʿUmar did (something). I, Abu Bakr and ʿUmar set out.' So I hoped that Allah will keep you with both of them." I turned back to see that the speaker was ʿAli ibn Abi Talib.[410]

Imam Bukhari 🕮, also proves that in all reality Sayyiduna ʿAli wanted cared little about politics. We have from the Prophet's uncle al-Abbas 🕮, who comes to Sayyiduna ʿAli 🕮 to give him advice during the final illness of the Messenger of Allah 🕮. He said, "By Allah, after three days you will be a servant to the one in authority, And by Allah, I feel that the Messenger of Allah 🕮 will die from this current ailment he is enduring, for I know how the faces of the offspring of ʿAbdul-Muttalib look at the time of their death. So let us go to the Messenger of Allah 🌿 and ask him who will be in position of authority after his death. If the authority is given to us we will know as to it, and if it is given to somebody else, we will inform him so that he may tell the new ruler to take care of us." ʿAli said, "By Allah, if we asked the Messenger of Allah for it and he denied it us, the people will never give it to us after that. And by Allah, I will not ask the Messenger of Allah for it.' Truly, the Messenger of Allah, said, "We do not assign the authority of ruling to those who ask for it, nor to those who are keen to have it."[411]

The proof for this, is that Sayyiduna ʿAli had good relations with all of the first three Caliphs before him and was actually their vizier [*Wazir*].

On top of this they were all close friends with some even naming children after one another. For example Sayyiduna ʿAli raised Sayyiduna Abu Bakr's son after his death, so this notion of disputes between the 3 Caliphs and Sayyiduna ʿAli is a false one indeed, invented by those who love to split up communities.

Here ends the book the Virtues of ʿAli ibn Abi Talib 🌿.

Much more can be said, however brevity is the Sunnah and with Allah is the Success.

I hope you enjoyed the Jewels from the Virtues of the Life of Sayyiduna ʿAli ibn Abi Talib 🌿.

The first and last of the calls is Alhamdulillah.

Endnotes

1. Surah al-Araf, Quran, 7:43

2. Surah Hud, Quran, 11:41

3. Surah Aali Imran, Quran, 3:56

4. Related by Abu al-Qasim al-Taymi in al-Targhib wa al-Tarhib, Intro, The Drink of the People of Purity by Imam al-Qandusi, Translated by Abdul Aziz Suraqah, Ibriz Media

5. Narrated by Imam Ahmad ibn Hanbal in his Musnad

6. Imam Ibn Abi Hatim and Ibn Asakir narrated this from the route of Akrama who narrated from ʿAbdullah ibn Abbas that 33:33 was also revealed regarding the blessed wives of Prophet. Imam as-Suyuti, Tafsir Durr al-Munthur, Volume 5, pg. 562 Note by author: Ikrama mistakenly believed that this verse was only in regard to the wives and he was mistaken in that.

7. Surah Hud, Quran, 11:73, An Angel approached Ibrahim's wife Sarah and said this to her. Therefore she was considered part of his family. Peace be upon them.

8. Surah an-Nisa', Quran, 4:69

9. Surah an-Nahl, Quran, 16:43, According to some of the opinions of the Mufasirun (Those who explain the Quran), the People of the Reminder are the Ahlul-Bayt themselves, and the proof of it being obligatory to love the family of the Prophet is within the Quran itself, in the Chapter of al-Shura' 42:23.

10. Surah ash-Shura', Quran, 42:23

11. This is the same Anas ibn Malik who narrated that for six months following the revelation of verse 33:33, every morning (while going for fajr salat), the Prophet used to knock at the door of Fatimah's house and loudly recite Ayah of Tatheer. (Surah al-Ahzab, Quran, 33:33)

12. Related by Imam Jalaludin as-Suyuti in his Ihya al-Mayyit Fi Fada'il Ahlul-Bayt. (translation by Sayyid Arfan Shah). He notes that this has been recorded in the commentaries of Ibn al-Mundhir, Ibn Abi Hatim and Ibn al-Murduwiyah & the Mu'jamul Kabir of Imam at-Tabarani. Imam Bukhari agrees with this position.

13. Surah al-An'am, Quran, 5:35

14. Imam as-Shafi'i, in his Diwan pg. 50; also Quoted by Imam Ahmad Ibn Hajar al-Haytami al-Shafi'i in his Khayrat Hisan pg. 69

15. Imam at-Tabrani Mujam ul-Awsat, 3/122 # 2251

16. On the authority of Abu Hurayrah, Imam Hakim narrated this in his alMustadrak alas' Sahihayn #5359 and says it is Sahih on the conditions set by the Imams Bukhari and Muslim; Hafiz Shamsudin ad-Dhahabi agrees with this and say in his Talkhis. "This Hadith is Sahih on the conditions set by Imam Muslim."

17. On the authority of ʿAbdullah ibn Abbas, Sunan at-Tirmidhi, the Chapter on Virtues – Book 49, Hadith #4158

18. It is weak, yet can be acted upon. It was related through Imam ibn Asakir by Ibn Addi in his al-Kamil 5/243, Intro to Shaykh Yusuf Nabhani's Endless Nobility of the Ahlul-Bayt, translated by Sayyid Arfan Shah

19. Sahih Bukhari The Chapter on the Virtues of the Companions, #3541.

20. Imam at-Tabarani says in his al-Kabir that this Hadith is Sahih. Imam as-Shawkani agrees with this and it can be found in his Darrus Sahaba #210: "The narrators are Thiqat (trustworthy)."

21. Imam al-Hakim says in his Mustadrak alas' Sahihayn, Volume 3, pg 148. This Hadith is Sahih al-Isnad according to the conditions laid down by the Shaykhayn—Imams Bukhari & Muslim

22. al-Sawa'iq al-Muhriqah, by Imam Ahmad ibn Hajar al-Haythami, Chapter 9, Section 2. Shaykh al-Haythami says that the Messenger of Allah made this announcement during the Farewell Pilgrimage, on the day of Arafat, on the day of Ghadir Khum, on the return from Ta'if, also in Madinah from the pulpit, and in his deathbed.

23.   Al-Hakim, Mustadrak alas' Sahihayn, Volume 6, pg. 216; Mishkat al-Masabih, Volume 2 pg. 258; Hilyatul' Awliyah, Volume 4, pg. 306; Kanzul' Ummal, Volume 6, pg. 216; as-Sawa'iq al-Muhriqah, Commentary of Surah al-Anfal, 8:33 pg. 282 and many, many others. In another narration on the authority of ʿAbdullah ibn Abbas and ʿAbdullah ibn Zubayr the wording "drowned" is used instead of "doomed." This is in the Tafsir al-Kabir, Imam Fakhruddin ar-Razi, in his explanation of verse 42:23, Pt. 27, pg. 167; Some such as Imam ad-Dhahabi say this Hadith is weak, however Imam al-Hakim said otherwise and he lists it as Sahih upon the condition of Imam Muslim.What should be known is that sometimes Imam al-Hakim also makes mistakes in regard to the ranking of Hadith, he may say something when Sahih when upon further analysis it was not. Thus in these cases we wouldn't go with either of the rulings of Sahih or Daeef. In regard to this Hadith it is best to go with the ranking of Imam as-Suyuti who said in his al-Jami' as-Saghir, Volume 2 pg. 533. "This Hadith is a Hasan/good Hadith which is strengthened by multiple transmissions."

24.   Imam Jalaluddin as-Suyuti's Ad-Durr al-Manthur fi Tafsir bil-Ma'thur: The Scattered Pearls: Inter-textual Exegesis

25.   Surah al-Baqarah, Quran, 2:58

26.   Imam al-Hakim relates that ʿAli was born in the Kaba' in his Mustadrak alas' Sahihayn, Volume 4 pg. 197, Mullah ʿAli Qari al-Hanafi also has this opinion, as per his Sharh us-Shifa Volume 1 pg.327; ibn as-Sabbagh al-Maliki also relates the same in his Fusul al-Muhimmah pg.29 as well as many others.

27.   Bakkah is where Hagar and Isma'il settled after being taken by Ibrahim to the wilderness, a story also related in the Bible's Book of Genesis (21:14-21)

28.   Bakkah is the modern day city of Mecca, also known as Umm al-Quran or the mother of all settlements.

29.   Surah Aali Imran, Quran, 3:96

30.   Surah al-Baqarah, Quran, 2:125

31.   Surah Ibrahim, Quran, 14:37

32.   Surah Aali Imran, Quran, 3:90

33.   Surah Hud, Quran, 11:73

34.   Hadith No. 2630, Book of The Rites of Hajj, Sunan An-Nasa'i, Volume 3; Hadith # 2888, Chapters on Hajj, Sunan ibn Majah, Volume 4

35. Fatimah bint Asad bin Hashim bin Abd Munaaf. Was a beloved supporter of the Messenger of Allah and helped raise him after the death of his beloved parents. Her funeral prayer was performed by the Messenger of Allah, and he prepared her grave and prayer for her.

36. Whether Sayyiduna ʿAli was the only person ever born inside the Kaba or not, is not within the scope of the purpose of this book and thus the difference of opinion will be left alone.

37. ʿAbdullah ibn ʿAbd al-Muṭṭalib (Shaybah) ibn Hashim (ʿAmr) ibn ʿAbd Manaf (al-Mughira) ibn Qusayy (Zayd) ibn Kilab ibn Murra ibn Kaʾb ibn Luʾayy ibn Ghalib ibn Fahr (Quraysh) ibn Malik ibn an-Naḍr (Qays) ibn Kinanah ibn Khuzaymah ibn Mudrikah (ʿĀmir) ibn Ilyas ibn Muḍar ibn Nizar ibn Maʾād ibn ʿAdnan (553–570) was the father of the Prophet Muhammad. He was the son of Shaybah ibn Hashim (ʿAbdul-Muttalib), and was married to Aminah bint Wahb.

38. Tarikh at-Tabari, Volume 4 pg.303

39. Surah ad-Duha, Quran, 93:6-8

40. The History of at-Tabari, Tarikh at-Tabari Volume. 4 pg. 584

41. The History of at-Tabari. Albany: State University of New York Press. 1988. pg.44.

42. ʿAqeel ibn Abi Talib was the second oldest son of Abu Talib, born ten years after Talib and he, Aqeel, became Muslim during the year of the conquest of the city of Mecca, Hijaz. (Fath al-Mecca)

43. Seerah ibn Hisham, Cairo Edition pg. 146; Dalaʾil an-Nubuwwyah by Imam al-Bayhaqi, Volume 2 pg. 101

44. Khazanat al-Adaab by Hafiz al-Khatib al-Baghdadi, Volume 1 pg. 261; Tarikh of Hafiz ibn Kathir, Volume 3 pg. 42; Fath al-Bari Sharah of Sahih Bukhari, Volume 7 pg. 153; Al-Isabah, Volume 4 pg. 116 and others

45. Musnad of Imam Ahmad 6/118

46. Some say the Messenger of Allah took in ʿAli because of Abu Talib's finances and there is an opinion that Rasul Allah and Khadijah wanted to adopt ʿAli at the time after the loss of their son al-Qasim. Allah always Knows best.

47. Adapted from the Seerah of ibn Hisham Volume 1 pg. 163, This is also related in the Tarikh at-Tabari Volume 2 pg. 63, Seerah ibn Kathir, Musnad of Imam Amad ibn Hanbal and many others

48. Imam Abu Nuaym's Hilyatul Awliyah, Volume. 1, pg. 67; also related in the Tafsir ad-Durr al-Manthur by Imam as-Suyuti

49. As-Seerah an-Nabawiyyah, pg. 177

50. Muruj adh-Dhahab, Volume 2/283

51. The Life of Sayyidah Zainab, the Hero of Karbala

52. Hafiz ibn as-Salah in section 39, pg.178, of his Muqaddimah mentions some of the differing views as follows: "The pious predecessors differed over who was the first of them to accept Islam. Some said Abu Bakr as-Siddiq and this is conveyed from Ibn Abbas, Hasan ibn Thabit, Ibrahim an-Naka'i and others. Some said 'Ali was the first to accept Islam. This is conveyed from Zayd ibn Arqam, Abu Dhar, al-Miqdad and others".

53. Sunan at-Tirmidhi ~ Kitab al-Manaqib ~ Book 49, Hadith 4094

54. Al-Kamil ibn Athir, pg.43

55. Quran 33:72; 33 ways of developing Al-Khushu'

56. Shaykh Ahmad ibn Ajiba's Tafsir Fatiha al-Kabir, Beirut: Dar al-Kutub al-'Ilmiyya, 2004, pg. 244

57. Surah al-Ma'eda, Quran, 5:55

58. Imam at-Tabari, Tafsir, Volume 6, pg. 165; Imam Fakhrudin ar-Razi, Tafsir al-Kabir Volume 3, pg. 431.

59. Surah ash-Shu'ara, Quran, 26:214

60. The Life of the Prophet Muhammad, Seerah Nabawiyyah, Volume 1 pg. 264, This is also related in multiple biographies of the Prophet.

61. Imam at-Tabari relates this story in his History of at-Tabari, Volume 2 pg. 62

62. This is not to be confused with thinking that Sayyiduna 'Ali was to be the first Caliph. This honor was given to Sayyiduna Abu Bakr as-Siddiq and his leadership is confirmed upon by consensus.

63. Imam at-Tabari, at-Tarikh, Volume 1 pgs. 171-173; Imam al-Bayhaqi, Dala'il an-Nubuwwa, Volume. 1 pgs. 428-430; Imam Jalaluddin as-Suyuti, ad-Durru al-Manthur, Volume 5 pg. 97; and many others

64. Surah al-Inshirah, Quran, 94:5-6

65. Surah al-Ankabut, Quran, 29:2

66. Seerah, Volume 1 pg. 350-351

67. The Life of the Prophet Muhammad by Muhammad Husayn Haykal, Cairo, 1935

68. Related by ibn Hisham, ibn Ishaq, Hafiz ibn Kathir, Imam Jalaluddin as-Suyuti and others

69. Surah al-Anam:162-163

70. The History of Tabari, Tarikh at-Tabari, Volume 4 pg. 301

71. Sahih Bukhari 4/81 8/168; Sahih Muslim 3/1420

72. Sunan Abu Dawud 5/103; Sunan at-Tirmidhi 5/194; Sunan an-Nasa'i 101 and Sunan ibn Majah 1/73

73. Musnad Ahmad 3/390

74. Surah Tawbah, Quran, 9:51

75. Surah as-Saff, Quran, 61:8

76. Surah al-Baqarah, Quran, 2:207

77. Imam ibn Hisham lists the plotters and those who were to execute this assassination plot as: Abu Jahl, Hakam bin Abil Al-'As, ʿUqbah bin Abi Mu'ait, An-Nadr bin Harith, Umayyah bin Khalaf, Zama'a bin Al-Aswad, Tu'ayma bin ʿAdi, Abu Lahab, Ubay bin Khalaf, Nabih bin Al-Hajjaj and his brother Munbih bin Al-Hajjaj

78. Quran, Surah Ya-sin, 36:9

79. For more info one can look into the Seerah Ibn Hisham, Volume 1/483

80. Surah Tawbah, Quran, 9:40

81. Quran, Surah an-Nisa, 4:58

82. Surah al-An'am, Quran, 6:33

83. Surah al-Ahzab, Quran, 33:6

84. Sahih Bukhari & Muslim

85. Abu Ayyub al-Ansari is from the Banu an-Najjar. His full name is Khalid ibn Zayd ibn Kulayb.

86. Surah Tawbah, Quran, 9:117

87. Surah Tawbah, Quran, 9:71

88. Surah Tawbah, Quran, 9:100

89. Sahih Bukhari, The Book of the Merits of the Helpers of Madinah, Volume 5, Book 58, Number 128

90. Sunan at-Tirmidhi

91.   Quote from the Messenger of Allah in Seerah ibn Hisham

92.   Zubayr accepted Islam at the hands of Abu Bakr as-Siddique. He made the Hijrah to al-Habasha and attended all of the battles of the Prophet. He gained the nickname of the "Disciple of the Prophet" during the Battle of the Trench. After deciding to leave the battle against ʿAli ibn Abi Talib he was followed and martyred at the hands of ʿAmr ibn Jurmuz.

93.   Sir William Muir ~ The Life of Muhammad, London, 1877

94.   Badr is the name of a well and a market-place of Arabia, it is about 80 miles from Madinah, and is so named after a certain Badr bin Quraish bin Mukhlad bin an-Nadr bin Kananah, who hailed from the clan of the Bani Ghaffar.

95.   Sahih Hadith in Sahih Muslim, Quran 20:130

96.   Tarikh at-Tabari, Volume 7 pg. 31

97.   Narrated by Abu Ishaq from Haritha ibn Mudharrib, Musnad of Imam Ahmad ibn Hanbal #1042; also related by Abu Yaʼla #302, #412

98.   Al-Maghazi, the Battles, Oxford Printing

99.   Phillip Hitti, the History of the Arabs

100.   Ibn Sʼad relates this in his at-Tabaqat al-Kubra from Qatada.

101.   Sunan Abu Dawud

102.   Sir John Glubb, The Great Arab Conquests, 1963

103.   Surah al-Anfal, Quran, 8:5-8

104.   Surah Aali Imran, Quran, 3:123-127

105.   Muʼjam Al-Kabir

106.   On the authority of Al-Miswar bin Makhramah, Sahih Bukhari – The Book of the Companions of the Prophet—Book 62, Hadith #64

107.   Sunan at-Tirmidhi, The Book of Manaqib, Book 49, Hadith #4150

108.   Imam al-Hakim narrated in his Mustadrak #4721 on the authority of Hudayfah ibn Yaman. Hafiz ad-Dhahabi said this Hadith is Sahih.

109.   Quote in parenthesis is from the Hilyatul-Awliyah' ~ The Beauty of the Righteous—Volume 1/34 and others

110.   Sahih Bukhari, Book #40, Hadith #563

111.   Musnad of Imam Ahmad, Sunan at-Tirmidhi

112.　Imam Bukhari's Adab al-Mufrad, the Book of Greetings

113.　Sunan an-Nasa'i, the Book of Marriage

114.　Sunan an-Nasa'i, the Book of Marriage, It is said that the Messenger of Allah asked Bilal ibn Rabah to sell Imam Ali's shield for him. After he did, ʿAli divided the money into three sections. A part of it was given to Bilal ibn Rabah to purchase a decent perfume for ʿAli and Fatimah, and then ʿAli spent the other two to purchase some household items and clothes for his newly wedded wife.

115.　Sahih Bukhari, the Book of Gifts, Book 51, Hadith #46

116.　Sahih Bukhari: Volume 7, Book 64, Hadith Number 275.

117.　On the authority of ʿAbdullah ibn Abbas, Recorded by Imam Ahmad ibn Hajar al-Haythami in his Majma'u-Zawaid 9/205; Note: This is related by Imam at-Tabarani and its narrators are Thiqat (strong and trustworthy).

118.　Sahih Muslim Volume 4, The Merits of Fatimah

119.　Related by Imam at-Tabarani in al-Majma al-Awsat (3:137#2721); Imam Ahmad ibn Hajar al-Haythami in his Majma az-Zawa'id (19:201) said that Imam at-Tabarani and Abu Yala also transmitted it and its chain of narrators is sahih (sound); Imam Shawkani, Darr-us-Sahabah fi-Manaqib al-Qarabah was-Sahabah (pg. 277 #24)

120.　Imam al-Hakim, al-Mustadrak (3:168#4736); Ibn Abi Shaybah, al-Musannaf (7:432#37045); Shaybani, al-Aahad wal-Mathani (5:360#2952); Ahmad bin Hanbal, Fadail-us-sahabah (1:364#532); al-Khatib al-Baghdadi, Tarikh Baghdad (4:401). No worries this of course was not in a private setting, we seek refuge in Allah from any such kind of misguided interpretations.

121.　Sahih Bukhari, The Book of the Virtues and Merits of the Prophet and his Companions

122.　Sahih Hadith narrated on the authority of ʿAbdullah ibn ʿUmar, Sunan ibn Majah

123.　Hasan Hadith narrated by Abu Hurayrah, Sunan ibn Majah, #143

124.　The names of the children between Fatimah and ʿAli are: al-Hassan, al-Husayn, Zaynab, Umm Kulthum and Muhsin.

125.　Sunan at-Tirmidhi, The Book of Sacrifices, the Adhan in the Ear of the Newborn

126.　Muwatta of Imam Malik, The Book of Aqeeqa

127. Muwatta of Imam Malik, the Book of Aqeeqa

128. Imam at-Tabarani related from this the route of Salim that Abi al-Ju'd.

129. Ibn al-Athir in Asad al-Ghabah

130. Sahih Hadith , Sunan at-Tirmidhi

131. Hasan Gharib Hadtih, Sunan at-Tirmidhi

132. Hasan Sahih Hadith, Sunan at-Tirmidhi

133. Related by Imam al-Hakim in his al-Mustadarak alas' Sahihayn

134. Mustadrak Alas' Sahihayn of Imam al-Hakim Al-Nisaburi, 2/385 Sunan Al-Bayhaqi, 3/376 Al-Tabari, 2/514

135. The Message, The Story of Islam, 1977. Directed by Moustapha Akkad, Written by H.A.L Craig, Tewfik El-Hakim, A.B Jawdat el-Sahrar, A.B Rahman el-Sharkawi and Muhammad Ali Maher

136. Surah Aali Imran, Quran, 3:153

137. Surah Aali Imran, Quran, 3:152

138. Sahih Muslim, the most of famous of the martyrs in this incident may be be Abu Dujana . Ibn Hisham in his Seerah said: Abu Dujana, he is the one who protected the Messenger of Allah from arrows being shot by the Quraysh, he made his body a shield.

139. Seerah ibn Hisham, Seerah ibn Ishaq. Imam Bukhari also agrees this story and relates it in his Sahih.

140. Sahih Bukhari, Volume 4, Book 52, Number # 159, The Book of Struggle and Expeditions

141. Surah Aali Imran, Quran, 3:172-174

142. Tafsir Ibn Kathir Juz' 21 (Part 21): Surah Al-Ankabut 46

143. Surah al-Ahzab, Quran, 33:10-11

144. Surah al-Ahzab, Quran, 33:13

145. Sahih Bukhari, Book 59. Number 424

146. Sahih Bukhari, Military Expeditions led by the Prophet (Al-Maghaazi)Volume 5, Book 59, Number 425

147. Surah al-Ahzab, Quran, 33:9

148. Surah al-Ahzab, Quran, 33:25

149. Sahih Muslim, Sahih Bukhari, The Book of Peacemaking, Volume 3, Book 49, Number 862

150. Imam al-Bukhari recorded in his Sahih in ʿBook of Conditions'

151. Sahih al-Bukhari, #2731, 2732

152. Sahih Bukhari, Volume 4, Book 52, Hadith #253

153. Sahih Muslim, Book 19, Number 4450

154. Majmu az-Zawa'id, Volume 9/131

155. Related in the Sunan of Imam ibn Majah, Volume. 1, pg. 83, Hadith #117

156. az-Zarkani, Volume 2, pg. 230, Imam as-Suyuti's The History of the Righteous Caliphs, Tarikh al-Khulafa, pg. 33

157. Sawa'iq al-Muhriqah, The Loud Lightning

158. Imam Jalaluddin ar-Rumi, Mathnawi, trans. R. A. Nicholson, Lahore. Volume 1 pg .202.

159. Martin Lings

160. The Book of Certainty, Cambridge, 1992. Chapter The Sun and the Moon

161. Edward Gibbon, The Decline and Fall of the Roman Empire

162. This event happened on the 4th of Dhul Qada, the 11th month of the Islamic Hijri Calendar in the year (4 A.H) (629 CE.)

163. Hafiz ibn Hajar al-Asqalani, Fath Al-Bari, 7/700

164. Sahih Bukhari, Volume 5 , Book 59, Hadith #700; Sa'd also narrates this as is related by Imam Muslim in his Sahih, Book 31, Hadith #5916. This Hadith is Mutawattir as well.

165. Tarikh at-Tabari 9:51; Tarikh ibn Athir 1:341; Seerah ibn Hisham 946-7; Seerah ibn Ishaq 604; Tarikh ibn Kathir 5:11

166. It is important to note that just as Jesus had to deal with an extreme group among the Jews, namely the Pharisees, ʿAli had to also deal with an extreme group the Khawarij. What this means is that they were groups that were literal. They would take the law and only look at the outer (Zaahir), without any reflection or commentary.

167. The Loud Lightning – as-Sawa'iq al-Muhriqah by Shaykh Ahmad ibn Hajar al-Haythami

168. Sunan of Imam an-Nasa'i

169. The History of Tabari, Tarikh at-Tabari, 9:58-59

170. Points on the life of Sayyiduna ʿAli—Related by Shaykh G.F Haddad –www.sunnah.org/publication/khulafa_rashideen/caliph4.htm

171. Fage, J. D., A History of Africa (London: Routledge, 2001), pp. 53–4.

172. A. F. L. Beeston; Some Observations on Greek and Latin Data Relating to South Arabia in Bulletin of the School of Oriental and African Studies, University of London, Volume. 42, No. 1 (1979), pgs. 7-12

173. Ibn Ishaq, The Life of Muhammad, (Oxford, 1955), 657–58

174. Seerah al Halabi, Volume 3, pg. 239.

175. Tafsir ibn Kathir, Ayat of Mubahala

176. According to the Tarikh of al-Yaqubi, Volume 2/66; Ibn Ishaq and many others, Sixty of the most distinguished and wise men of Najran were selected for the purpose.

177. Surah Aali Imran, Quran, 3:61

178. Imam Zamarkashi's Kashshaf, Volume 1, pgs. 282-283; Imam Fakhrudin ar-Razi, Tafsir-i Mafatihul Ghayb, Volume 2, pgs. 481-482; Ibn Athir Tarikh al-Kaamil, Volume 2, pg. 112

179. Tafsir Ibn Kathir Juz' 3 (Part 3): Surah Al-Baqarah 253 to Surah Aali-'Imran 92 2nd Edition, MSA Publication Ltd, pg. 125

180. Surah al-Baqarah, Quran, 2:257

181. Surah al-Furqan, Quran, 25:57

182. Surah al-An'am, Quran, 6:50. Parts 1-30 of Bidayat as-Sul fi Tafdil ar-Rasul, The Beginning of the Quest for the High Esteem of the Messenger. By Imam Izz ibn Abd al-Salam, Translated by Aisha Bewley pg. 23

183. Surah ar-Ra'd, Quran, 13:7

184. Surah al-Baqarah, Quran, 2:189

185. Surah an-Nisa', Quran, 4:59

186. Sunan at-Tirmidhi, Book 47, Hadith 3441, In other Versions #3148 #3615, #3616

187. Surah Aali Imran, Quran, 3:31

188. Surah an-Nisa', Quran, 4:59

189. Surah Bayyinah, Quran, 98:7

190. Surah Luqman, Quran, 31:23

191. Kitab as-Shifa bi Tarif Huquq al-Mustafa, Section 4: Regarding the Signs of Love for the Prophet

192. Surah Tawbah, Quran 9:24

193. Sahih al-Bukhari, Volume 1, Book 2, Hadith #14

194. Qadi Iyad's Kitab ash-Shifa bi Tareef Huquq al-Mustafa Chapter Two, Section 1: Regarding the Necessity in Loving the Prophet

195. Surah an-Nisa', Quran, 4:80

196. Shamail at-Tirmidhi pg. 21

197. Surah al-Ahzab, Quran, 33:21

198. Fath al-Bari, Explanation of the Sahih of Imam Bukhari, 2/421

199. Mathnawi of Imam Jalaluddin ar-Rumi, 1/161

200. Sahih al-Bukhari, Volume 4, Book 56, Number 759

201. The Messenger of Allah taught this Dua to his daughter Fatimah az-Zahra. Related in the Sunan al-Kubra an-Nasa'i, Volume 6/147 on the authority of Anas ibn Malik

202. Surah al-Ankabut, Quran, 29:69

203. Surah Ya-Sin, Quran, 36:21

204. Surah Tawbah, Quran, 9:119

205. Muwatta of Imam Malik, The Book of Speech, Book 56, Hadith #1830

206. Ta'lim al-Muta'alim by Imam Burhan ad-Din az-Zarquni

207. The Sublime Revelations, Al-Fathur Rabbani, pg. 202

208. Surah Aali Imran, Quran, 3:103

209. On the authority of Abu Abdullah an-Numan ibn Bashir. Sahih Bukhari & Muslim; Riyadus Saliheen of Imam Nawawi Hadith # 6

210. Sahih Muslim, The Book of Enjoining Good Manners, Book 45, Hadith 41

211. Surah Maryam, Quran, 19:97

212. Surah Taghabun, Quran, 64:11

213.   Surah al-Mujadilah, Quran, 58:22

214.   On the authority of Abdullah ibn Amr ibn al-Aas, Sahih Muslim, Volume 4, pg.1397, # 6418. It is also narrated by Umm Salamah and there are different variations of this Hadith as well. For example it is also reported by Imam Ahmad ibn Hanbal on the authority of the mother of the believers Aisha.

215.   Khasa'is Sayyiduna ʿAli ibn Abi Talib by Imam an-Nasa'i, the author of Sunan al-Kubra an-Nasa'i

216.   Surah al-Hadid, Quran, 57:3

217.   Mawsu'at of Imam Ibn Abi Dunyah 1/174, Kitab al-Matar war-R'ad wal-Barq

218.   Surah Muhammad, Quran, 47:19

219.   Surah al-Ambiya, Quran, 21:25

220.   A number of people have narrated this from Ahmad ibn Muhammad ibn Khalid from Ahmad ibn Muhammad ibn Abu Nasr from Abul Hasan al-Muwasalli from Abu Abd Allah. Usul al-Kafi, Volume 1, Chapter 31, Hadith #6

221.   Mujalasah wa Jawahir al-Ilm

222.   Sidi Ahmad Ibn Ajiba in Miraj at-tshwafa Haqiaq at-Tassawaf p.55

223.   Surah al-Qassas, Quran, 28:88, Here Allah is telling us that He is Eternal, Ever Lasting, Ever Living, Self-Sustaining, Who, although His creation dies, He will never die.

224.   Sahih Bukhari and Muslim

225.   The Hikam of ibn Ata'illah al-Iskandari

226.   Related by Imam al-Hakim an-Nishapuri

227.   Tarikh, Ibn Askir, Volume 2 pg. 488; Kanz al Ummal, Volume 5 pg. 33

228.   Al-Muttaqi al-Hindi's Kanz ul-Ummal; al-Hakim, Mustadrak al Hakim, Volume 3 page 123

229.   Sahih Muslim; 40 Hadith of Imam Nawawi; Sunan ibn Majah, Chapters on Slaughtering and others

230.   Surah Rahman, Quran, 55:60

231.   Surah al-Mu'minun, Quran, 23:14

232. Musnad of Imam Ahmad # "Khasais" (#111) narrated from Abdullah ibn Nujay who is weak according to the Hadith masters.

233. Imam Hakim also narrated this in his Mustadrak #4630, Khasa'is of Imam an-Nasa'i #116,117

234. Surah al-Qasas; 83; Reported by Imam at-Tabari in his 'Jami' al-Bayan'; 20/122

235. Related by Imam Abu Nuaym in Hilyah al-Awliyah, Volume 1, pgs. 65-66; Kanz al-'Ummal Volume.12, pg. 214 by Shaykh al-Muttaqi al-Hindi

236. Mustadrak alas' Sahihayn, al-Hakim ~ Volume 2, pg.135

237. Al-Jami' ul-Ahkam ul-Quran; Imam al-Qurtubi, 17/256; Imam al-Qurtubi related this and then for some reason says it is weak, however, the Hadith master Imam al-Hakim said that these narrations are Sahih as per standard of the two Shaykhs = Imam Bukhari and Muslim and Imam Dhahabi although strict in Hadith agreed upon that

238. Sunan at-Tirmidhi, 13/178; Ibn Al-Maghazeli, 122; Asad Al-Ghaba, 4/26; Al-Riyadh An-Nudhra, 2/216.

239. Mustadrak alas' Sahihayn of al-Hakim, 3/109; Musnad of Imam Ahmad, 4/370; al-Khasa'is of Imam an-Nisa'i, 25; Sunan at-Tirmidhi; at-Tabarani.

240. Al-Hakim, Mustadrak alas' Sahihayn, Volume 3, pg. 121, quotes this tradition and says, "It is authentic according to the methods of verification followed by both Shaykhs Imam Bukhari & Muslim, however they did not record it." It is also recorded on pg. 73 of Imam as-Suyuti's book Tarikh al-Khulafa, on pg. 24 of Imam an-Nasai's Khasais, and on pg. 82 of al-Khawarizmi's book Al-Manaqib.

241. Musnad of Ahmad, 5/94; Mustadrak As-Sahihayn of Al-Hakim An-Nisaburi, 3/128; Kanz Al-Umal, 6/217; also Related by Imam at-Tabarani

242. Mustadrak Al-Sahihayn of Al-Hakim Al-Nisaburi, 2/241; Tarikh Baghdad of Al-Khatib Al-Baghdadi, 6/85

243. Sahih Hadith in the Sahih of Imam Bukhari; Sunan ibn Majah

244. Sahih Bukhari

245. Fath al-Bari, Explantion of Sahih Bukhari 7/507

246. Al-Manaqib of Ibn Al-Maghazeli, 243; Tarikh al-Baghdad of Hafiz Khatib Al-Baghdadi, 4/410; Al-Jami' of Imam as-Suyuti, 2/145

247. Kanz Al-Umal, 6/122; Recorded by Imam at-Tabari, 2/201; Al-Khawarizmi, 250; al-Fada'il of Ahmad, 253; Ibn Al-Maghazeli, 42/200.

248. Sunan of Imam at-Tirmidhi, al-Mustadrak alas Sahihayn of Imam al-Hakim an-Nishapuri, Volume 3 pgs. 126-127, Ad-Durar al-Muntatharah fi al-Ahadith al-Mushtahirah by Imam Jalaluddin as-Suyuti, pg. 23; ʿAbdullahi ibn ʿAbbas also narrated this and it can be found related by Imam al-Hakim and Imam Tabarani's, ʿMaujam Al Awsat', The Greater Collection

249. Mullah Ali Qari says, It is proven that The Hadith of ʿI am the city of knowledge and ʿAli is its gate' was narrated by Imam al-Hakim in the Kitab al-Manaqib in his al-Mustadrak from ʿAbdullahi ibn ʿAbbas. Imam al-Hakim goes on to say that his is a Sahih Hadith. Imam ad-Daraqutni said: This is a proven (thabit) Hadith, and Imam at-Tirmidhi narrated it Hadith in his Kitab al-Manaqib in his al-Jami'. ~ Al-Mirqat fi Sharh al-Mishkat, ʿAli al-Qari, Volume. 5, pg. 571

250. Hafiz ibn Hajar said: The truth of this Hadith is that it has a degree of sound (Hasan), it is not raised to rigorously authentic nor is it to be degressed to a forgery.

251. as-Sawa'iq al-Muhriqa, The Loud Lighting by Imam Ahmad ibn Hajar al-Haytami al-Makki , pg. 122. He said both versions of the above Hadith were existent in the Sunan, one of Imam at-Tirmidhi's works.

252. The History of Damascus, Tarikh Dimashq Volume 42 pg. 408

253. Khasa'is Sayyiduna ʿAli by Imam an-Nasa'i, # 111 pg. 9; This is also related in the Tarikhul Khulafa of Imam as-Suyuti in a slightly different form on the authority of Imam al-Hakim.

254. Sunan al-Kubra, Al-Manaqib, pg. 83, Hadith # 70; & pg. 311, Hadith # 309

255. Futuhat al-Makkiyah, Imam Abdul Wahhab as-Sharani relates something similar in his Yawaqit wal-Jawahir on the authority of Muhyidin ibn al-Arabi

256. Good/Hasan Hadith related by Imam an-Nasa'i in al-Khasais #71; Sunan ibn Majah #119; Sunan at-Tirmidhi in #3719

257. Sunan at-Tirmidhi, Volume 1, pg. 38; Miskhat Sharif, Volume 2, pg. 8; Musnad of Imam Ahmad ibn Hanbal, Volume 1, pg. 146

258. Sahih Bukhari, Chapter 69. Book of the Virtues of the Qur'an, translated by Aisha Bewley

259. Siyar Alam an-Nubala', The Lives of the Noble Figures, Section on the Schools of Tafsir pg. 39

260. Sahih Hadith related in al-Mustadarak alas' Sahihayn, Volume 3, pg.

134, Hadith 226/4628. Imam Ahmad Ibn Hanbal said it is a Sahih Hadith on the authority of Abu Sa'id al-Khudri

261.   Al-Arqam was from the Makhzum clan of the Quraysh tribe. His father, known as Abi'l-Arqam, was Abd Manaf ibn Asad ibn Umar ibn Makhzum. His mother was Umayma bint Al-Harith from the Khuza'a tribe. He accepted Islam at the hands of Sayyiduna Abu Bakr as-Siddique, and married Hind bint Abdullah from the Banu Asad.

262.   Surah al-Anbiya, Quran, 21:107

263.   Surah an-Najm, Quran, 53:3-4

264.   Surah an-Nahl, Quran, 16:44

265.   Surah al-Isra', Quran, 17:82

266.   Sunan Ibn Majah (Muqaddima, #211), Sunan ad-Darimi (#3192), Imam Ahmad (#11831, 11844, 13053), at-Tayalisi (#2238), Abu Nu'aym (3:63, 9:40), Imam an-Nasa'i (Sunan al-Kubra, #8031), Imam al-Hakim (1:556 Sahih), Imam al-Bayhaqi (Shu'ab, #2688-89), Hakim at-Tirmidhi (Nawadir, Asl #67), al-Khatib in his Tarikh (2:311, 5:357), Harith (Zawa'id, p. 229 #732), and Imam Daylami in Firdaws (1:494 #1649). See also: Hafiz Sakhawi (Maqasid, #249), Hafiz ʿAjluni (Kashf al-Khafa' #16, #768, #811). It is Sahih, according to Imam as-Suyuti (Jami' as-Saghir, #2374) and Mundhiri (Targhib wa Tarhib, 2:354).

267.   Surah Yusuf, Quran, 12:111

268.   Tafsir at-Tabari, Volume 1 pg. 80

269.   Durr al-Manthur fi Tafsir Bil-Ma'thur , The Scattered Pearls Intertextual   Exegesis

270.   Surah an-Nisa', Quran, 4:82

271.   The Way of the Quran by Khuram Murad

272.   Surah al-Isra', Quran, 17:106

273.   Surah al-Hashr, Quran, 59:19

274.   Surah al-Ahzab, Quran, 33:34

275.   Surah Tawbah, Quran, 9:6

276.   Sunan of Imam at-Tirmidhi, Musnad of Imam Ahmad ibn Hanbal

277.   Sahih Bukhari, a similar narration can be found on the authority of ʿUthman ibn ʿAffan

278.   Musnad of Imam Ahmad Sunan at-Tirmidhi

279. Sahih Bukhari and Muslim, Riyadus Salihin of Imam an-Nawawi The Gardens of the Righteous

280. Surah al-Baqarah, Quran, 2:2

281. Sahih, Hadith in his al-Mustadarak alas' Sahihayn, Volume 3, pg. 134, Hadith 226/4628. Imam Ahmad Ibn Hanbal said it is a Sahih Hadith from Abu Said al-Khudri

282. Siyar Alam an-Nubala' pg 39, the Schools of Tafsir ~ The Lives of the Noble Figures

283. Related by Imam Jalaluddin as-Suyuti in his Tarikh al-Khulafa', ~ TheHistory of the Righteous Caliphs on pg. 173

284. al-Mustadrak alas Sahihayn, by Imam al-Hakim, Volume 3, pg, 112, who wrote that this is an authentic Hadith with a sound chain of narration from Anas ibn Malik, according to the conditions set by the two Hadith masters = Imam Bukhari and Muslim.

285. Fathul-Bari fi Sharh Sahih al-Bukhari, by Ibn Hajar al-Asqalani, Volume 10, pg. 386; al-Itqan, by al-Suyuti, Volume 1, pg.165; Hilyatul Awliyah, by Imam Abu Nu'aym al-Asbahi, Volume 1, pg. 67; Kanzul Ummal, by al-Muttaqi al-Hindi, Voume 15, pgs. 112-113; as-Sawa'iq al-Muhriqah, by Imam ibn Hajar al-Haythami, Chapter 9, Section 4, pg. 197; Ma'rifat al-Qurra' al-Kibar, by Hafiz ad-Dhahabi, Volume 1, pg. 31)

286. al-Burhan, by az-Zarkashi, Volume 1, pg. 259; al-Itqan, by Imam Jalaluddin as-Suyuti, Volume 1, pg. 202; Fathul Bari, by Hafiz ibn Hajar al-Asqalani, Volume 10, pg. 417

287. Naskh in relation to the Quran, is a substitution of one law for another. Allah makes an example in 2:106

288. Mansukh is that which has now been rejected and replaced by the above law.

289. Shaykh Ahmad Ibn Hajar al-Haythami, as-Sawa'iq al-Muhriqah, pg. 126; Imam Jalaluddin as-Suyuti, al-Itqan, Volume 1, pg. 59

290. Tabaqat al-Kubra by ibn Sa'd, Volume 1 pg. 204

291. Kitab al-Luma fee at-Tasawwuf, The Book of the Light of Spirituality pg. 129

292. Sahih in Sanad, related in the Mustadarak alas' Sahihayn of Imam al-Hakim; Volume 3,pg. 133, narration # 4624; Imam Ahmad ibn Hajar al-Haythami says concerning this. Its Riwayah/chain of narration and its people are strong. = Majmu' az-Zawa'id Volume 9 pg.135; also considered

Sound according to Imam at-Tabarani in his Mu'jam al-Awsat, Volume 6 pg. 162, as narrated on the authority of ibn ʿUmar.

293. Musnad of Ahmad, 5/94; Mustadrak alas' Sahihayn of Imamal-Hakim Al-Nisaburi, 3/128; Kanz Al-Umal, 6/217; Also related by Imam at-Tabarani.

294. Hafiz ibn Kathir, Tafsir Quran al-Azim 7/413

295. Hilyatul-Awliyah by Imam Abu Nu'aym Volume 1, pgs. 67-68; Tabaqat al-Kubra by ibn Sa'd, Volume 2, pg. 101; Kanzul-Ummal by Shaykh al-Muttaqi al-Hindi, Volume 15, pg., 113; as-Sawa'iq al-Muhriqah, by Shaykh Ahmad Ibn Hajar al-Haythami, Chapter. 9, Section 4, pg.197

296. al Riyadh al-Nadirah, Volume 2 pg. 198; Tarikh, as-Suyuti, pg. 124; al-Itqan, as-Suyuti, Volume 2 pg. 319; Fath al-Bari, Volume 8 pg. 485

297. Surah Qaf, Quran, 50:37

298. Surah al-Mujadila, Quran, 58:11

299. Surah al-Baqarah, Quran, 2:269

300. Sunan of Imam at-Tirmidhi, al-Mustadrak alas Sahihayn of Imam al-Hakim an-Nishapuri, Volume 3 pgs. 126-127, Ad-Durar al-Muntatharah fi al-Ahadith al-Mushtahirah by Imam Jalaluddin as-Suyuti, pg. 23; ʿAbdullah ibn ʿAbbas also narrated this and it can be found related by Imam al-Hakim and Imam Tabarani's, ʿMaujam Al Awsat', The Greater Collection

301. Mullah Ali Qari says, It is proven that The Hadith of ʿI am the city of knowledge and ʿAli is its gate' was narrated by Imam al-Hakim in the Kitab al-Manaqib in his al-Mustadrak from ʿAbdullah ibn ʿAbbas. Imam al-Hakim goes on to say that his is a Sahih Hadith. Imam ad-Daraqutni said: This is a proven (thabit) Hadith, and Imam at-Tirmidhi narrated it Hadith in his Kitab al-Manaqib in his al-Jami'. ~ Al-Mirqat fi Sharh al-Mishkat, ʿAli al-Qari, Volume. 5, pg. 571

302. Hafiz ibn Hajar said: The truth of this Hadith is that it has a degree of sound (Hasan), it is not raised to rigorously authentic nor is it to be digressed to a forgery.

303. as-Sawa'iq al-Muhriqah, The Loud Lighting by Imam Ahmad ibn Hajar al-Haytami al-Makki , pg. 122. He said both versions of the above Hadith were existent in the Sunan, one of Imam at-Tirmidhi's works.

304. Imam al-Bayhaqi's Shu'ab al-Iman, The Branches of Faith, Volume 12 pg. 195

305. Hafiz ibn Kathir, Tafsir Quran al-Azim

306.   Imam an-Nawawi narrated a remarkable chain for a Hadith going back to ʿAli: "Among the best of the narrations of the type of sons from fathers is that of al-Khatib with a chain going back to ʿAbd al-Wahhab ibn ʿAbd al-ʿAziz ibn al-Harith ibn Asad ibn al-Layth ibn Sulayman ibn al-Aswad ibn Sufyan ibn Yazid ibn Akina al-Tamimi who said: I heard my father say: I heard my father (Sufyan) say: I heard my father (al-Aswad) say: I heard my father (Sulayman) say: I heard my father (al-Layth) say: I heard my father (Asad) say: I heard my father (al-Harith) say: I heard my father (ʿAbd al-ʿAziz) say: I heard my father (ʿAbd al-Wahhab) say... This is also related in Imam Abu Nuaym's Hilyatul Awliyah, Volume 1, 100-128

307.   Al-Munqih min al-Dalal, The Deliverance from Error

308.   Kanz al-Ummal fi Sunan wal Aqwat wal Afwal, Volume 1 pg. 96

309.   The Scales of Wisdom, 877

310.   Imam Abu Nu'aym, Hilyatul' Awliyah, The Adornment of the Friends of Allah pg. 75

311.   Mishkat al-Anwar ~ Bab Fi Zimmi Dunyia

312.   Surah Yunus, Quran, 10:35

313.   Surah Hud, Quran, 11:47

314.   Kanzul Ummal, Volume 5 pg. 241 by al-Muttaqi al-Hindi

315.   Surah al-Baqarah, Quran, 2:32

316.   Surah al-Ma'eda, Quran, 5:48

317.   Surah Yunus, Quran, 10:59

318.   Surah an-Nahl, Quran, 16:116

319.   Musnad of Imam Ahmad ibn Ahmad ibn Hanbal, Hayatus' Sahaba, The Lives of the Companions

320.   Surah Nur, Quran, 24:51

321.   Surah az-Zumar, Quran, 39:18

322.   He is a Hadith Master, one of the greats. Muhammad ibn Munkadir (died 747), also known as Ibn al-Munkadir or Muhammad al-Taymi, was a prominent follower of the Sahaba. He was also known for his recitation of the Qur'an, and one who transmitted a number of Hadith < Mashahir, 65; Abu Nu'aym, in. 146-58

323.   Al-Madkhal ila Sunan al-Bayhaqi

324.   Sunan of Imam ad-Darimi, Hilyatul Awliyah of Imam Abu Nu'aym al-Asbahani, The Adornment of the Friends of Allah

325. Surah az-Zumar, Quran, 39:9

326. Surah Yunus, Quran, 10:35

327. Related by Imam al-Ajurri in Akhlaq Al-'Ulamah # 45, also related by Hafiz al-Khatib al-Baghdadi in Al-Faqih wal-Mutafaqqih, Volume. 2 pgs. 338-339

328. Sahih Bukhari, the Chapter about a person preferring some people with certain knowledge to the exclusion of others.

329. Fath al-Bari, the explanation of Sahih Bukhari

330. Sahih of Imam Muslim

331. Sahih Bukhari, Kitab al-Adab the Book of Good Manners

332. On the authority of Abu Musa al-Ashari, Sunan Abu Dawud, Kitab al-Adab, the Book of Good Manners

333. Sunan ibn Majah #154

334. This is Sahih: Related by Imam al-Hakim in his Mustadrak #5328; Imam Abu Nuaym in his Hilyatul' Awliyah 1/65 and Ibn Sad in his Tabaqat al-Kubra 2/339

335. The History of the Righteous Caliphs, Tarikh al-Khulafa' by Imam Jalaluddin as-Suyuti

336. Also related Hafiz ibn Hajar al-Asqalani in his at-Tahthib pg.337, ibn Hajar in his al-Isabah, Volume 2 pg. 509, Imam Ahmad ibn Hanbal in his Musnad and Imam Abu Nu'aym al-Isfahani in his Hilyatul Awliyah, Ibn Hajar Asqalani in his Tahdheeb at-Tahdeed, printed in Hyderabad Daccan, page 337; Ibn Hajar in Isaba, Volume II, printed in Egypt, page 509; Ibn Qutayba Dinawari in Ta'wil-e-Mukhtalafu'l-Hadith, page 201-202, Ibn Hajar Makki in Sawa'iq-e-Muhriqa, page 78; Hajj Ahmad Afindi in Hidayatu'l-Murtab, page 146 and 152; Ibn Athir Jazari in Usudu'l-Ghaiba, Volume IV, page 22; Jalalu'd-Din Suyuti in Ta'rikhu'l-Khulafa, page 66; Ibn Abdu'l-Birr Qartabi in Isti'ab, Volume II, page 474; Seyyed Mu'min Shablanji in Nuru'l-Absar, page 73 and many others

337. The Loud Lightning, as-Sawa'iq al-Muhriqah by Shaykh Ahmad ibn Hajar al-Haythami

338. Tabaqat al-Kubra ibn Sad, Volume 2 pg. 338

339. Al-Faqih wal-Muttafaqih by, Hafiz al Khatib al-Baghdadi, Volume 2 pg. 351

340. al-Jami Bayan al' Ilm wa Fadlihi by Hafiz Yusuf ibn Abd al-Barr al-Andalusi, Volume 1, pg. 383

341. Kanz-ul-Ummal pg. 48.

342. at-Tabari, Jami' al-Bayan fi Ta'wilil-Quran (also known as Tafsir Tabari, Volume 29, pg. 31

343. The History of Damascus by Imam Ibn ʿAsakir. Volume 42, pg. 299 and pg. 398

344. Surah al-Baqarah, Quran, 2:269

345. Kitab al-Ilal by the Muhaddith ʿAli ibn al-Madani

346. He is a Hadith Master, one of the teachers of Imam Bukhari

347. Kitab al-Ilal by the Muhaddith ʿAli ibn al-Madani

348. Tadhkira al-Huffaz, The Memorial of the Hadith Masters by Imam ad-Dhahabi

349. Mathnawi of Imam Jalaluddin ar-Rumi (3787)

350. Translated by Shaykh Abu Alfa ʿUmar Muhammad Shareef ibn Farid of the Sankore Institute of Islamic and African Studies

351. Hans Wehr Arabic Dictionary

352. Oxford Arabic Dictionary

353. Musnad of Imam Ahmad ibn Hanbal 5/94; Mustadrak alas-Sahihayn of Imam al-Hakim Volume 3/128 and others

354. Sahih Hadith in the Sunan at-Tirmidhi

355. Surah Yunus, Quran, 10:62-63

356. Related by Imam an-Nasa'i in his as-Sunan al-Kubra, 96, No. 79, the Section on the Virtues of ʿAli

357. al-Bidayah wa an-Nihayah by Hafiz ibn Kathir, Volume 5 pg. 229

358. Imam Ahmad bin Hanbal related this his Musnad (4:281); Imam ibn Abi Shaybah did do in his al-Musannaf (12:78 # 12167); as well as many others.

359. Imam Ahmad bin Hanbal related this Hadith from Bara' bin ʿAzib through two different chains of transmission in al-Musnad (4:281); as well as Imam Ibn Abi Shaybah, al-Musannaf (12:78 # 12167); Hafiz Ibn Kathir in al-Bidayah wan-Nihayah (4:169; 5:464) Imam Ibn ʿAsakir, Tarikh Dimashq al-Kabir (5:167, 168) and Imam Dhahabi has said in Siyar ʿA'lam an-Nubala' (2:623, 624) and others.

360. Surah al-Ma'eda, Quran, 5:67

145

361. Surah al-Ma'eda, Quran, 5:3

362. Sahih al-Bukhari, Arabic-English, traditions 5.688, 7.458, and 9.539

363. Imam Abu al-Qasim ibn Asakir, Tarikh Madinah wa Dimashq (Beirut: Dar al-Fikr; 1415 H), Volume 13, pgs. 69-70

364. Surah az-Zuhruf, Quran, 43:57

365. Abu Hurayrah's name is ʿAbdur Rahman ibn Sakhr ad-Dawsi al-Azdi. He is said to have memorized (almost all by heart) and narrated approx. 5,374 Ahadith after spending three years learning from the Messenger of Allah.

366. Sahih Muslim, The Book of the Virtues of Jesus the son of Maryam

367. This comparison to Jesus is very important, because it is as if the Messenger of Allah was telling him something. Meaning to live the example of the life of Jesus, which if you look at it, he did. So much so, that even some around him looked at him as a god, while others spoke of the displeasure that the revelation did not come down to ʿAli. It was a very trying time for our master.

368. Musnad of Imam Ahmad ibn Hanbal, The position not suited for him means that he was not a Prophet, nor Allah as some sects claim.

369. The Loud Lightning – as-Sawa'iq al-Muhriqah by Shaykh Ahmad ibn Hajar al-Haythami

370. Surah al-Isra, Quran, 17:71

371. Surah an-Nahl, Quran, 16:89

372. Hafiz ibn Kathir in his the Beginning and the End, Al-Bidayah wan Nihayah, Volume 7 pg. 359

373. Sunan at-Tirmidhi, Book of Virutes, Book 49, Hadith #4280

374. Surah al-Anfal, Quran, 8:72

375. Tarikh Ibn Asakir, 42/355

376. The Loud Lighting, as-Sawa'iq al-Muhriqah of Imam Ahmad ibn Hajar al-Haythami pg. 429

377. Kanz ul-Ummal, Volume 5 pg. 34

378. Please note that Sayyiduna ʿUmar ibn al-Khattab was a Caliph for ten years. In this time he conquered 140,000 square miles of land. Sayyiduna ʿAli advised him on many occasions regarding his rule, acting as his vizier.

379. Tarikh al-Islam, The History of Islam by Imam ad-Dhahabi

380. Tadhkira of Hafiz ibn Jawzi pg. 23

381. Sahih Bukhari, Volume 5, Book 57, #54

382. Imam Ibn Asakir, Tarikh Dimishq al-Kabir (14:61); Hindi, Kanz-ul-Ummal (12:98#34167); al-Haythami, Majma az-Zawa'id (9:174); az-Zurqani, Sharh-ul-Muwatta (4:443); ibn Hajr al-Asqalani, Lisan-ul-Mizan (2:94) Narrates it from Abu Musa al-Ashari with same wordings

383. al-Muhib at-Tabari has narrated this tradition in his Dhakhair-ul-Uqba fi Manaqib Dhaw-il-Qurba (pg.126), and says that Ibn Samman has mentioned it in his book al-Muwafaqah. He also narrated it in ar-Riyad-un-Nadrah fi Manaqib-il-Ashrah (3:128).

384. Good/Hasan Hadith narrated on the authority of Hudayfah. Sunan at-Tirmidhi, Book 49, Hadith 4023

385. Sahih Hadith, Sunan Abu Dawud, Book 42, Model Behavior of the Prophet Hadith 34

386. Ibn Asakir in his "Arbain fi manaqib ummahatil muminin" (#24) and he said it is a Hasan Sahih Hadith

387. Sahih Bukhari Hadith #3728

388. Sahih Hadith narrated by Ibn Umar & Abu Dharr, collected by Imams Ahmad, at-Tirmidhi and Abu Dawud.

389. Tabaqat ibn Sa'd, Volume 3 pg. 121

390. Surah al-Fath, Quran, 48:29

391. Mishkat al-Masabih from Sahih al-Bukhari and Muslim, 553

392. Fada'il as-Sahaba wa Manaqibihim wa Qawl Ba'adihim fi Ba'ad" by Imam Darqutni, the author of Sunan Darqutni

393. Sahih Bukhari, #683; Sahih Muslim, #418

394. Al-Isabah (Volume 1 pgs. 4-5) of al-Hafiz ibn Hajar.

395. Surah al-Ahzab, Quran, 33:57

396. Related by Imam at-Tirmidhi, also by Imam Ahmad with three good chains in his Musnad, Imam al-Bukhari in his Tarikh, Imam al-Bayhaqi in Shuʿab al-Iman, and others. Imam Jalaluddin as-Suyuti declared it to be a Hasan Hadith in his Jamiʿ as-Saghir #1442

397. Surah Aali Imran, Quran, 3:110

398. Surah Tawbah, Quran, 9:100

399. Sharh Sahih Muslim

400. Sahih of Imam Muslim

401. The Loud Lightning, as-Sawa'iq al-Muhriqah of Imam Ahmad ibn Hajar al-Haythami, pg.91

402. Related by Imam ad-Darqutni

403. This was mentioned by Al-Yaqubi and Al-Masudi, who both are Shia historians in their books = Tarikh al-Yaqubi, 2/228; an-Nateejah wal-Ishraf, pg.82

404. Al-Khatib al-Baghdadi made Takhrij for this in his "al-Kifayah" pg. 376 and said it is Sahih. It is narrated through other chains as well, it is Thabit.

405. Manaqib al-Imam Ahmad pg. 170

406. Aqeedah at-Tahawiyyah

407. Surah al-Fath, Quran, 48:29

408. The History of Damacus, ibn Asakir, Tarikh Dimashq, 42/235

409. al-Musannaf of Imam ibn Abi Shaybah

410. Sahih Bukhari, Book #57, Hadith # 26

411. Sahih Bukhari, the Book of Judgments